Crystal Reports 9:
Advanced

Instructor's Edition

THOMSON

™

COURSE TECHNOLOGY

Australia • Canada • Mexico • Singapore
Spain • United Kingdom • United States

Crystal Reports 9: Advanced

VP and GM of Courseware:	Michael Springer
Series Product Managers:	Caryl Bahner-Guhin and Adam A. Wilcox
Developmental Editor:	Jim O'Shea
Keytester:	Bill Bateman
Series Designer:	Adam A. Wilcox
Cover Designer:	Steve Deschene

For more information contact:

Course Technology
25 Thomson Place
Boston, MA 02210

Or find us on the Web at: www.course.com

For permission to use material from this text or product, contact us by

- Web: www.thomsonrights.com
- Phone: 1-800-730-2214
- Fax: 1-800-730-2215

Trademarks

Course ILT is a trademark of Course Technology.

Some of the product names and company names used in this book have been used for identification purposes only and may be trademarks or registered trademarks of their respective manufacturers and sellers.

Disclaimer

Course Technology reserves the right to revise this publication and make changes from time to time in its content without notice.

ISBN 0-619-20387-0

Printed in the United States of America

1 2 3 4 5 PM 06 05 04 03

Contents

Introduction   **iii**

Topic A: About the manual.. iv
Topic B: Setting student expectations viii
Topic C: Classroom setup... x
Topic D: Support... xii

Complex reports   **1-1**

Topic A: Parameter fields 1-2
Topic B: Subreports 1-13
Unit summary: Complex reports 1-22

Formatting complex reports   **2-1**

Topic A: The Section Expert 2-2
Topic B: Objects 2-14
Unit summary: Formatting complex reports 2-20

Advanced formulas and functions   **3-1**

Topic A: Variables... 3-2
Topic B: Advanced functions 3-12
Topic C: Constructs 3-18
Topic D: Running totals 3-25
Unit summary: Advanced formulas and functions............................. 3-29

Advanced data access techniques   **4-1**

Topic A: Dictionaries... 4-2
Topic B: ODBC data sources.. 4-12
Topic C: Crystal SQL Designer 4-16
Topic D: Report alerts.. 4-28
Unit summary: Advanced data access techniques............................ 4-33

Charts and maps   **5-1**

Topic A: Working with charts 5-2
Topic B: Working with maps... 5-11
Unit summary: Charts and maps 5-18

Course summary   **S-1**

Topic A: Course summary... S-2
Topic B: Continued learning after class S-3

Quick reference   **Q-1**

Index   **I-1**

Crystal Reports 9: Advanced

Introduction

After reading this introduction, you will know how to:

A Use Course Technology ILT manuals in general.

B Use prerequisites, a target student description, course objectives, and a skills inventory to properly set students' expectations for the course.

C Set up a classroom to teach this course.

D Get support for setting up and teaching this course.

Topic A: About the manual

Course Technology ILT philosophy

Our goal at Course Technology is to make you, the instructor, as successful as possible. To that end, our manuals facilitate students' learning by providing structured interaction with the software itself. While we provide text to help you explain difficult concepts, the hands-on activities are the focus of our courses. Leading the students through these activities will teach the skills and concepts effectively.

We believe strongly in the instructor-led classroom. For many students, having a thinking, feeling instructor in front of them will always be the most comfortable way to learn. Because the students' focus should be on you, our manuals are designed and written to facilitate your interaction with the students, and not to call attention to manuals themselves.

We believe in the basic approach of setting expectations, then teaching, and providing summary and review afterwards. For this reason, lessons begin with objectives and end with summaries. We also provide overall course objectives and a course summary to provide both an introduction to and closure on the entire course.

Our goal is your success. We encourage your feedback in helping us to continually improve our manuals to meet your needs.

Manual components

The manuals contain these major components:

- Table of contents
- Introduction
- Units
- Course summary
- Quick reference
- Index

Each element is described below.

Table of contents

The table of contents acts as a learning roadmap for you and the students.

Introduction

The introduction contains information about our training philosophy and our manual components, features, and conventions. It contains target student, prerequisite, objective, and setup information for the specific course. Finally, the introduction contains support information.

Units

Units are the largest structural component of the actual course content. A unit begins with a title page that lists objectives for each major subdivision, or topic, within the unit. Within each topic, conceptual and explanatory information alternates with hands-on activities. Units conclude with a summary comprising one paragraph for each topic, and an independent practice activity that gives students an opportunity to practice the skills they've learned.

The conceptual information takes the form of text paragraphs, exhibits, lists, and tables. The activities are structured in two columns, one telling students what to do, the other providing explanations, descriptions, and graphics. Throughout a unit, instructor notes are found in the left margin.

Course summary

This section provides a text summary of the entire course. It is useful for providing closure at the end of the course. The course summary also indicates the next course in this series, if there is one, and lists additional resources students might find useful as they continue to learn about the software.

Quick reference

The quick reference is an at-a-glance job aid summarizing some of the more common features of the software.

Index

The index at the end of this manual makes it easy for you and your students to find information about a particular software component, feature, or concept.

Manual conventions

We've tried to keep the number of elements and the types of formatting to a minimum in the manuals. We think this aids in clarity and makes the manuals more classically elegant looking. But there are some conventions and icons you should know about.

Convention/Icon	Description
Italic text	In conceptual text, indicates a new term or feature.
Bold text	In unit summaries, indicates a key term or concept. In an independent practice activity, indicates an explicit item that you select, choose, or type.
`Code font`	Indicates code or syntax.
`Longer strings of ▶ code will look ▶ like this.`	In the hands-on activities, any code that's too long to fit on a single line is divided into segments by one or more continuation characters (▶). This code should be entered as a continuous string of text.
	In the left margin, provide tips, hints, and warnings for the instructor.
Select **bold item**	In the left column of hands-on activities, bold sans-serif text indicates an explicit item that you select, choose, or type.
Keycaps like (↵ ENTER)	Indicate a key on the keyboard you must press.
	Next to an instructor note, indicates a warning for the instructor.
	Next to an instructor note, indicates a tip the instructor can share with students.
	Next to an instructor note, indicates a setup the instructor can use before delivering a step or activity.

Instructor notes.

⚠ *Warnings prepare instructors for potential classroom management problems.*

TIPS ✔ *Tips give extra information the instructor can share with students.*

🎲 *Setup instructor notes give a context for instructors to share with students.*

Hands-on activities

The hands-on activities are the most important parts of our manuals. They are divided into two primary columns. The "Here's how" column gives short directions to the students. The "Here's why" column provides explanations, graphics, and clarifications. To the left, instructor notes provide tips, warnings, setups, and other information for the instructor only. Here's a sample:

Do it!

A-1: Creating a commission formula

Take the time to make sure your students understand this worksheet. We'll be here a while.

Here's how	Here's why
1 Open Sales	This is an oversimplified sales compensation worksheet. It shows sales totals, commissions, and incentives for five sales reps.
2 Observe the contents of cell F4	F4 ▼ **=** =E4*C_Rate
	The commission rate formulas use the name "C_Rate" instead of a value for the commission rate.

For these activities, we have provided a collection of data files designed to help students learn each skill in a real-world business context. As they work through the activities, students will modify and update these files. Of course, students might make a mistake and therefore want to re-key the activity starting from scratch. To make it easy to start over, students will rename each data file at the end of the first activity in which the file is modified. Our convention for renaming files is to add the word "My" to the beginning of the file name. In the above activity, for example, students are using a file called "Sales" for the first time. At the end of this activity, they would save the file as "My sales," thus leaving the "Sales" file unchanged. If a student makes a mistake, he can start over using the original "Sales" file.

In some activities, however, it may not be practical to rename the data file. Such exceptions are indicated with an instructor note. If students want to retry one of these activities, you will need to provide a fresh copy of the original data file.

PowerPoint presentations

Each unit in this course has an accompanying PowerPoint presentation. These slide shows are designed to support your classroom instruction while providing students with a visual focus. Each one begins with a list of unit objectives and ends with a unit summary slide. We strongly recommend that you run these presentations from the instructor's station as you teach this course. A copy of PowerPoint Viewer is included, so it is not necessary to have PowerPoint installed on your computer.

Topic B: Setting student expectations

Properly setting students' expectations is essential to your success. This topic will help you do that by providing:

- Prerequisites for this course
- A description of the target student at whom the course is aimed
- A list of the objectives for the course
- A skills assessment for the course

Course prerequisites

Students taking this course should be familiar with personal computers and the use of a keyboard and a mouse. Furthermore, this course assumes that students have completed the following courses or have equivalent experience:

- *Crystal Reports 9: Basic*

Target student

Students will get the most out of this course if they want to learn how to use Crystal Reports 9 to create reports that accept user input, display subreports, and contain section formatting and advanced formulas. Students will also learn how to use Crystal Dictionaries, ODBC, and SQL queries, and how to use charts and maps.

Course objectives

You should share these overall course objectives with your students at the beginning of the day. This will give the students an idea about what to expect, and will help you identify students who might be misplaced. Students are considered misplaced when they lack the prerequisite knowledge or when they already know most of the subject matter to be covered.

After completing this course, students will know how to:

- Create and use parameter fields to accept user input; create and use edit masks and pick lists for parameter fields; and create and use subreports.
- Arrange field objects by adding, merging, and deleting report sections; and add hyperlinks and OLE objects.
- Use variables, arrays, and ranges in formulas; create formulas that use multiple functions; use Evaluation Time functions to determine when a formula is evaluated; use For and While constructs to control the execution of statements in a formula; and create and modify running totals.
- Use dictionaries to create and modify views of relevant data; use ODBC to access data from different types of databases; use Crystal SQL Designer to create SQL queries; and create, modify, and delete report alerts.
- Create and customize charts and maps to display report data graphically and geographically.

Skills inventory

Use the following form to gauge students' skill levels entering the class (students have copies in the introductions of their student manuals). For each skill listed, have students rate their familiarity from 1 to 5, with five being the most familiar. Emphasize that this is not a test. Rather, it is intended to provide students with an idea of where they're starting from at the beginning of class. If a student is wholly unfamiliar with all the skills, he or she might not be ready for the class. A student who seems to understand all of the skills, on the other hand, might need to move on to the next course in the series.

Skill	**1**	**2**	**3**	**4**	**5**
Creating and using parameter fields					
Using an edit mask in a parameter field					
Creating and using a pick list in a parameter field					
Creating and using subreports					
Adding, merging, and deleting report sections					
Adding hyperlinks					
Adding OLE objects					
Using variables and arrays					
Using ranges					
Creating a formula that uses multiple functions					
Using Evaluation Time functions					
Using For and While constructs					
Creating and modifying running totals					
Creating and modifying dictionaries, and creating reports from them					
Using ODBC to access different types of databases					
Using Crystal SQL Designer to create SQL queries					
Using queries to create reports					
Creating, modifying, and deleting Report Alerts					
Creating and modifying charts					
Creating and customizing maps					

Topic C: Classroom setup

All our courses assume that each student has a personal computer to use during the class. Our hands-on approach to learning requires that they do. This topic gives information on how to set up the classroom to teach this course. It includes minimum requirements for the students' personal computers, setup information for the first time you teach the class, and setup information for each time that you teach after the first time you set up the classroom.

Student computer requirements

Each student's personal computer should have:

- A keyboard and a mouse.
- Intel Pentium II or higher (Intel Pentium III or higher preferred).
- A minimum of 128 MB RAM or higher.
- A minimum of 320 MB free hard disk space.
- A CD-ROM drive to install the software.
- An SVGA or higher-resolution monitor.
- A floppy disk drive.
- A printer driver. The printer driver that was installed while this book's units were developed is HP LaserJet 4050 Series PCL 6.
- Internet access is required if you will be downloading data files from www.courseilt.com.

First-time setup instructions

The first time you teach this course, you will need to perform the following steps to set up each student computer.

1 Install Windows 2000 Professional Edition according to the software manufacturer's instructions. Perform a typical setup, accepting all of the default settings. (You can also use Windows XP, Windows 98, or Windows Millennium Edition, although the screen shots in this course were taken using Windows 2000, and students' screens might look somewhat different.)

2 Set the monitor's color depth to High Color (16 bit). Here's how:

   a Right-click a blank area of the desktop to display the shortcut menu. Then, choose Properties to open the Display Properties dialog box.

   b Activate the Settings tab.

   c From the Colors list, select High Color (16 bit).

   d Click OK. (If necessary, restart the computer.)

   Note: If you use a color setting other than High Color (16 bit), the program interface might not appear exactly as described or pictured in this book.

3 Do a Custom installation of Microsoft Office 2000 Professional. Install only Microsoft Word, Microsoft Excel, Microsoft Access, Office Tools, and Converters and Filters.

4 Do a Custom installation and install all the features of Crystal Reports 9 Professional Edition. When the Crystal Decisions Registration Wizard dialog box appears, click Register Later.

5 Install a printer driver. If possible, use the HP LaserJet 4050 Series PCL 6 driver.

6 Download the Student Data examples for the course. You can download the student data directly to student machines, to a central location on your own network, or to a disk.

   a Connect to www.courseilt.com/instructor_tools.html.

   b Click the link for Crystal Reports to display a page of course listings, and then click the link for Crystal Reports 9: Advanced.

   c Click the link for downloading the data disk files, and follow the instructions that appear on your screen.

7 Install Crystal Reports 9 Data Compatibility tools, which include the Crystal Reports Dictionary and SQL Designer tools. To do this:

   a Download the Crystal Reports 9 Data Compatibility tools from http://support.crystaldecisions.com/communityCS/FilesAndUpdates/ cr9_data_tools.zip.asp. This web address is not case sensitive.

   b Unzip the file.

   c Double-click cdq.exe to start the installation.

   d In the Crystal Data Compatibility Tools Setup wizard, click Next.

   e Select I accept the License Agreement and click Next.

   f Enter the user information and click Next.

   g Under Select Installation Type, select Complete and click Next.

   h Click Next to start the installation.

   i Click Finish to complete the installation.

Setup instructions for every class

Every time you teach this course, you will need to perform the following steps to set up each student computer.

1 If necessary, reset any defaults that have been changed in previous classes.

2 Delete the contents of the Student Data folder, if necessary. If this is the first time you are teaching the course, create a folder called Student Data at the root of the hard drive.

3 Copy the data files for the course to the Student Data folder (see the instructions in the preceding section about how to download the data files.)

Topic D: Support

Your success is our primary concern. If you need help setting up this class or teaching a particular unit, topic, or activity, please don't hesitate to get in touch with us. Please have the name of the course available when you call, and be as specific as possible about the kind of help you need.

Phone support

You can call for support 24 hours a day at (888) 672-7500. If you do not connect to a live operator, you can leave a message, and we pledge to return your call within 24 hours (except on Saturday and Sunday).

Web-based support

The Course ILT Web site provides several instructor's tools for each course, including course outlines and answers to frequently asked questions. To download these files, go to www.courseilt.com/instructor_tools.html. For additional Course ILT resources, including our online catalog and contact information, go to http://www.course.com/ilt.

Unit 1

Complex reports

Unit time: 65 minutes

Complete this unit, and you'll know how to:

A Use parameter fields to preview data based on specified criteria.

B Create and use subreports to display data from another report.

Topic A: Parameter fields

Explanation

Crystal Reports has several advanced features—including parameter fields and subreports—that offer users the flexibility to view only the data they need to see. For example, you can use parameter fields to preview data based on specified criteria. *Subreports* help users view data related to the primary report.

Ways to use parameter fields

A *parameter field* prompts the user to enter a value and then displays data based on that value. For example, a user might want to display sales data for only those years when product sales were greater than $100,000. You can create a parameter field that prompts the user to specify that or any other amount.

When creating a parameter field, you can specify a discrete value or a range of values. If you specify a *discrete value*, users can enter only a single value in the parameter field. However, if you use a *range*, users will be prompted to specify lower and upper limits for the parameter field. The report will then display the values that fall within the specified range. For example, to display sales between 2000 and 2002, a user can specify these years as the lower and upper limits of a range.

You can also use multiple parameter fields. For example, if you want to display data for the sales of a specific product in a specific year, you can create multiple parameter fields to prompt the user for this information.

There are several ways to use a parameter field, including:

- Placing it in the report
- Including it in a conditional formatting formula
- Including it in a record selection formula

To create a parameter field:

1   Open a report.
2   Choose View, Field Explorer to open the Field Explorer dialog box.
3   Select Parameter Fields.
4   Click New to open the Create Parameter Field dialog box.
5   Enter a name and prompting text for the parameter field, and then specify a value type. The name identifies the parameter field and will appear in the Field Explorer. The prompting text prompts the user to enter a value. The value type specifies the type of data that can be entered in the field, such as string, number, or datetime.
6   Click OK.

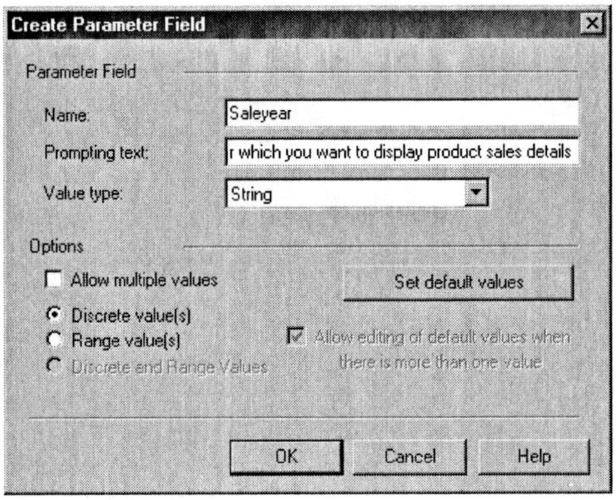

Create Parameter Field   ☒

Parameter Field

Name: Saleyear

Prompting text: r which you want to display product sales details

Value type: String   ▼

Options

☐ Allow multiple values   Set default values

⦿ Discrete value(s)
○ Range value(s)   ☑ Allow editing of default values when
○ Discrete and Range Values   there is more than one value

OK   Cancel   Help

Exhibit 1-1: The Create Parameter Field dialog box

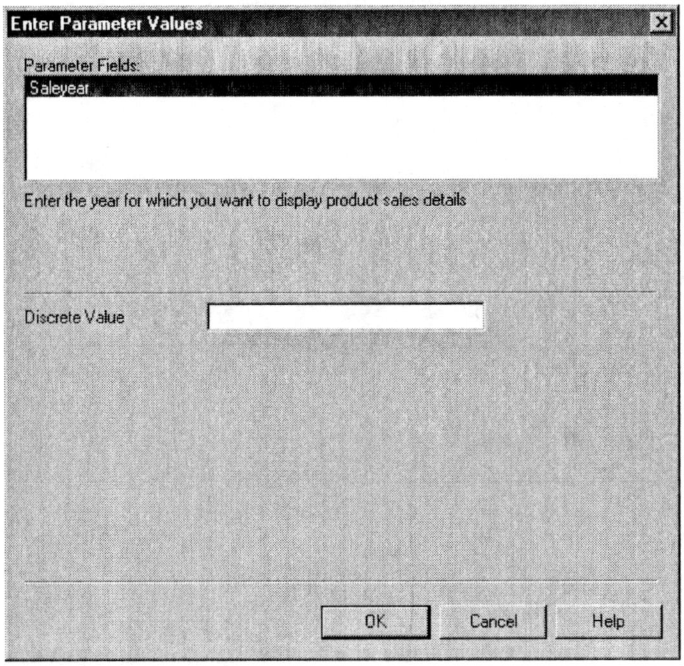

Enter Parameter Values   ☒

Parameter Fields:

Saleyear

Enter the year for which you want to display product sales details

Discrete Value

OK   Cancel   Help

Exhibit 1-2: The Enter Parameter Values dialog box

Do it!

A-1: Creating a parameter field

Here's how	Here's why
1 Start Crystal Reports 9	Choose Start, Programs, Crystal Reports 9. The Welcome to Crystal Reports dialog box appears.
2 Clear **Show welcome dialog at startup**	
Click **OK**	The Open dialog box appears.
3 Open Products report	From the current unit folder.
Maximize the window	If necessary.
Observe the report	It shows product sales for several years. You'll create and use a parameter field to display the data for only a specific year.
4 Choose **View**, **Field Explorer**	To open the Field Explorer.
From the list, select **Parameter Fields**	
Click 🗐	(The New button is on the toolbar in the Field Explorer.) To open the Create Parameter Field dialog box.
5 In the Name box, enter **Saleyear**	To specify a name for the parameter field.
In the Prompting text box, enter **Enter the year for which you want to display product sales details**	To specify the text that will appear in the dialog box that prompts the user for the parameter field value.
In the Value type list, verify that String is selected	(As shown in Exhibit 1-1.) This is the parameter field's data type.
Click **OK**	Saleyear is added to Parameter Fields in the Field Explorer dialog box.

If the Registration Wizard appears, tell students to click Register Later.

⚠ *If you want to refresh report data, you'll need to set the database location for the report. However, that is not necessary to perform this activity.*

📦 *Tell students that the Vice President of Sales wants to view product sales for a specific year.*

6 Choose **Report**, **Select Expert...**

To open the Choose Field dialog box.

Under Product detail, select **Year**

You'll apply the parameter value to the Year field.

Click **OK**

The Select Expert dialog box appears.

7 From the list, select **is equal to**

Another list appears.

From the second list, select **{?Saleyear}**

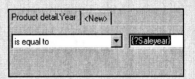

To specify that only those records with the year equal to the parameter value Saleyear appear when the report is previewed. The question mark (?) before the field name indicates that it is a parameter field.

Click **OK**

The Enter Parameter Values dialog box appears because you used a parameter field in the record selection formula, as shown in Exhibit 1-2.

8 In the Discrete Value box, enter **2001**

To display sales figures for the year 2001.

Click **OK**

A message box appears, asking if you want to use saved data or refresh the data.

Click **Use Saved Data**

Products Report			
Product ID	Product Name	Sales	Year
P001	Cinnamon ground	$4,000.00	2001
P010	Chervil	$2,000.00	2001
P012	Cumin	$1,200.00	2001
P017	Pepper	$5,000.00	2001
P019	Savoury	$1,500.00	2001
P020	Shallots	$1,200.00	2001

To display sales figures for 2001 only.

9 Save the report as **My products report**

In the current unit folder.

Edit masks

You use an *edit mask* for a parameter field to accept a user's input in a specific format. An edit mask limits the type of data that you can enter in a field. For example, you might create a report that prompts the user for an employee's Social Security number. Because Social Security numbers are displayed in a specific format (###-##-####, where # represents a number), you need to use an edit mask to ensure that the user enters the number in that format.

You can specify an edit mask only for fields using the String data type.

There are several characters that you can use to create an edit mask. These are called *masking characters*. The following table describes some of the masking characters:

Character	Description
A	The user can enter any alphanumeric character, but the character must be in the parameter value.
a	The user can enter any alphanumeric character but does not need to enter a character in place of the masking character "a."
L	The user can enter only letters and must enter a letter in place of the masking character.
C	The user can enter any character or space but does not need to enter a character or space in place of the masking character.
?	The user can enter only a letter but does not need to enter a letter in place of the masking character.
&	The user can enter any character or space and must enter a character or space in place of the masking character.
#	The user can enter any digit, a space, or a plus or minus sign but does not need to enter anything in place of the masking character.
9	The user can enter a number or a space but does not need to enter anything in place of the masking character.
0	The user can enter only numbers and must enter a number in place of the masking character.
\	The character entered after this appears as a literal. For example, if you specify the edit mask "0\L0," then the parameter value will consist of a digit, the letter L, and another digit. This character is useful only when you need to include a reserved masking character as a part of the parameter value.
<	The characters entered after this character are converted to lowercase.
>	The characters entered after this character are converted to uppercase.

Character	Description
Password	Here you specify the word "Password" for an edit mask. When you enter characters for this type of mask, asterisks (*) appear in place of the actual characters. This is useful for creating conditional formulas in which you specify that some fields of the report will appear only when a password is entered.
Separator characters	These include periods (.), commas (,), colons (:), semicolons (;), hyphens (-), and slashes (/). Other characters cannot replace these characters, and they form a part of the parameter value. For example, in the case of a Social Security number, the hyphens (-) cannot be replaced by other characters, and they form a part of the parameter value.

To apply an edit mask to a field:

1 Open the Create Parameter Field dialog box.

2 Specify a name, prompting text, and data type for the parameter field.

3 Click Set default values to open the Set Default Values dialog box.

4 In the Edit mask box, enter the masking characters.

5 Click OK to set the edit mask for the parameter field.

6 Click OK to create the parameter field. When you refresh the data in the parameter field, the Enter Parameter Values dialog box will display the edit mask in the Discrete Value box.

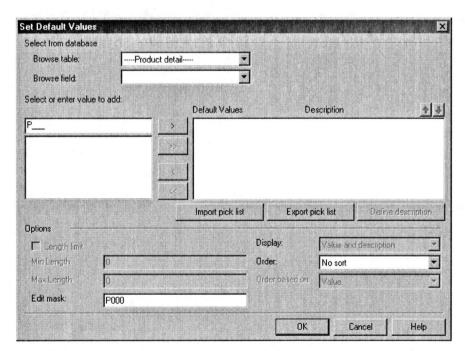

Exhibit 1-3: The Set Default Values dialog box

A-2: Applying an edit mask to a parameter field

Here's how	Here's why
1 Click 📇	(In the Field Explorer.) To open the Create Parameter Field dialog box.
In the Name box, enter **ProdID**	
In the Prompting text box, enter **Enter the Product ID for which you want to display sales details**	In the Value type list, String should be selected.
Click **Set default values**	To open the Set Default Values dialog box. You'll specify an edit mask for the field ProdID.
2 Under Options, in the Edit mask box, enter **P000**	
	Options ☐ Length limit Min Length Max Length Edit mask: P000
	This parameter field can now take only a string that starts with P and is followed by three numbers.
Observe the Select or enter value to add box	It shows "P___", as shown in Exhibit 1-3.
Click **OK**	To set the edit mask.
Click **OK**	ProdID is added to Parameter Fields.
3 Open the Select Expert dialog box	Choose Report, Select Expert.
Click **New**	The Choose Field dialog box appears.
Under Product detail, select **Product ID**	(If necessary.) You'll apply the ProdID parameter to this field.
Click **OK**	A Product detail.Product ID tab is added to the dialog box and is active.
4 From the list, select **is equal to**	
From the second list, select **{?ProdID}**	To view the records with the Product ID equal to the parameter field value.
Click **OK**	The Enter Parameter Values dialog box appears.

5 Place the insertion point as shown

| Discrete Value | P▌ |

P and a line appear in the box, indicating that an edit mask is applied to this field. The character P forms a part of the field value and cannot be changed.

Enter **00**

Click **OK**

Insert Parameter Field   ☒

⚠ This character should be a digit.

[OK]

A message appears because you have not entered all of the wanted digits. Because you specified three zeros in the edit mask as masking characters, you must enter three numbers.

Click **OK**   To close the message box.

6 Place the insertion point as shown

| Discrete Value | P00▌ |

If necessary.

Enter **1**   You'll view the records associated with Product ID P001.

Click **OK**   A message box appears, asking if you want to use saved data or refresh the data.

Click **Use Saved Data**

Products Report

Product ID	Product Name	Sales	Year
P001	Cinnamon ground	$4,000.00	2001

The data for the Product ID P001 and year 2001 appear in the report.

7 Update the report

Pick lists

A user who is previewing a report with a parameter field might not be aware of all the values the field contains. To provide the user with a list of default values, you can create a *pick list*. You can add values to the list from either an existing text file or a database field. By adding values from a field, you can provide the user with the exact field values. If you use a text file, you can add only those values that are stored in the file, which might differ from the exact values.

To get a list of values from a text file, you use the Import pick list button in the Set Default Values dialog box. To create a pick list from a database field:

1   Create a new parameter field. (You can also modify an existing parameter field.)

2   Open the Set Default Values dialog box.

3   From the Browse table list, select a table name.

4   From the Browse field list, select the field from which you want to create the pick list. A list of values will appear in the Select or enter value to add list.

5   Click Add All to add all the values to the Default Values list. You can also click the Add button to add selected values individually.

6   Click OK to close the Set Default Values dialog box.

7   Click OK to create the parameter field with the pick list. When you refresh the report data, the Discrete Values list in the Enter Parameter Value dialog box will contain the values from the pick list.

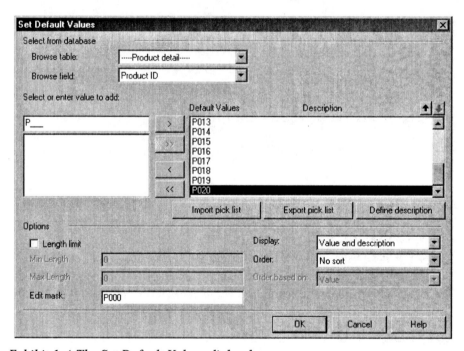

Exhibit 1-4:The Set Default Values dialog box

Do it!

A-3: Using a pick list in a parameter field

Here's how	Here's why
1 In the Field Explorer dialog box, verify that ProdID is selected	
Click ✎	(The Edit button is in the Field Explorer.) To open the Edit Parameter Field dialog box.
2 Click **Set default values**	(To open the Set Default Values dialog box.) You'll create a pick list for the parameter field ProdID.
From the Browse table list, select **Product detail**	The pick list will contain values from a field in this table.
From the Browse field list, select **Product ID**	To add values to the pick list from the Product ID field.
Observe the Select or enter value to add list	All the values of the Product ID field appear in the list.
3 Click ⟩⟩	Default Values P013 P014 P015 P016 P017 P018 P019 P020
	(This is the Add All button.) To add these values to the Default Values pick list for the parameter field. The dialog box should now look like Exhibit 1-4.
Click **OK**	To close the Set Default Values dialog box and set the pick list for the parameter field.
4 Click **OK**	To close the Edit Parameter Field dialog box.

🗄 *Tell students that when the Vice President of Sales views the report, he might not be aware of all the field values. To provide him with this information, they will create a pick list containing all possible values for the parameter field.*

TIPS ✓ *Tell students that they can also import a list of values stored in a text file by clicking the Import pick list button.*

TIPS ✓ *Tell students that they can also add selected values to the list by clicking the Add (>) button.*

TIPS *Tell students they can also press F5.*

5 Choose **Report**, **Refresh Report Data**

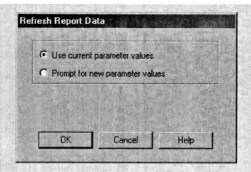

The Refresh Report Data dialog box appears.

Select **Prompt for new parameter values**

To specify a new value for the parameter field.

Click **OK**

The Enter Parameter Values dialog box appears. In the Parameter Fields list, Saleyear is selected.

6 In the Discrete Value box, enter **2002**

From the Parameter Fields list, select **ProdID**

P001 appears in the Discrete Value box. This is one of the values that you added to the pick list.

Display the Discrete Value list

Notice the range of values in the list.

Select **P011**

You'll need to scroll down the list.

Click **OK**

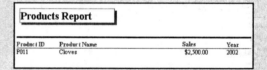

The report displays details for sales figures for Cloves (Product ID P011) in the year 2002.

7 Update and close the report

Topic B: Subreports

Explanation
When creating a report, you might want to display some related data from another report. For example, in an inventory stock report, you might need to add information about suppliers. To do this, you can create a subreport.

A *subreport* is a report that's contained within the primary or container report and cannot be previewed separately. There are two types of subreports: unlinked and linked. You can use an existing report as a subreport, or you can create a new one. When you insert a subreport, a new tab with the subreport name is added to the report window, in addition to the Design and Preview tabs.

When you want to add multiple subreports to a container report and you don't need to preview all of them simultaneously, you can add them as on-demand subreports. An *on-demand subreport* appears as a hyperlink in the container. You view the full subreport by clicking the hyperlink.

Unlinked subreports

An *unlinked subreport* is an independent report. Its data is not linked or coordinated with data in the container report, nor is any attempt made to match its records to those in the container report. To insert an unlinked subreport into a container report:

1 Open the report in which you want to insert the subreport.

2 Choose Insert, Subreport to open the Insert Subreport dialog box.

3 You can create a new subreport or insert an existing report:

- To insert an existing report, select Choose a report and specify the report file name.

- To create a new subreport, select Create a subreport, specify a report name, click Report Expert, and follow the prompts to complete the procedure.

4 If you want the subreport to appear as a hyperlink in the primary report, check On-demand subreport.

5 Click OK to create the subreport. The pointer will change to an arrow with a rectangular outline.

6 In the primary report, click the location where you want to place the subreport.

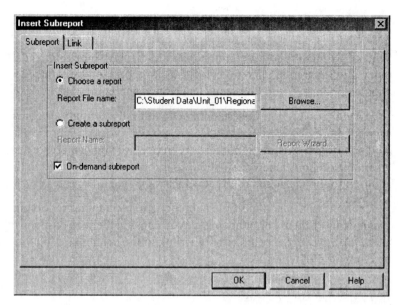

Exhibit 1-5: The Insert Subreport dialog box

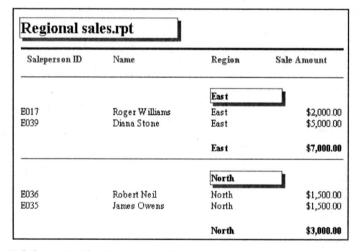

Exhibit 1-6: The Regional sales on-demand subreport

Do it!

B-1: Creating an unlinked subreport

Here's how	Here's why
1 Open Sales report	The Vice President of Sales wants to include sales details for each salesperson in the report. To accomplish this, you'll add an unlinked subreport to this report.
Activate the Design tab	
2 Choose **Insert**, **Subreport...**	To open the Insert Subreport dialog box. By default, the Subreport tab is activated.
Select **Choose a report**	You'll add an existing report as a subreport.
Click **Browse**	To display the Open dialog box.
Select **Regional sales**	From the current unit folder.
Click **Open**	The report name and its full path appear in the Report File name box.
Check **On-demand subreport**	To display the subreport as a hyperlink in the main report. The dialog box should look like Exhibit 1-5.
3 Click **OK**	
	The pointer changes to an arrow with a rectangular outline. You can click the mouse at the position where you want to place the subreport.
Click in the Report Footer section, as shown	
	To place the subreport in this section.
Observe the tabs	
	There is now a new tab with the subreport's name.
Deselect the subreport	Click anywhere in the container report.

If you want to refresh report data, you'll need to set the database location for the report. However, that is not necessary to perform this activity.

⚠️ *Make sure that students deselect the report. Otherwise, they won't be able to see the change in the pointer shape.*

4 Preview the report

(Click the Preview tab.) The subreport name appears in the container report.

5 Point to the subreport name, as shown

Regional sales.rpt

The pointer changes to a hand, indicating that this is a hyperlink to the subreport.

Click the hyperlink

The subreport appears under a new preview tab as shown in Exhibit 1-6.

6 Save the report as **My sales report**

Close the report

Linked subreports

Explanation

You might want to create a subreport in which the data changes based on what the user previews in the container report. For example, you might create a report that prompts the user for a year and displays that year's total cost, profit, and sales data. You can then add a subreport that displays the sales for each product for that year. Data in a *linked subreport* is coordinated with data in the primary report, and the records displayed in the subreport match those displayed in the main report. The two reports are linked on a common field.

To insert a linked subreport:

1   Open a report.
2   Open the Insert Subreport dialog box.
3   Verify that Create a subreport is selected. Then, specify a report name.
4   Click Report Wizard to open the Standard Report Creation Wizard dialog box.
5   Create the report, and click OK to return to the Insert Subreport dialog box.
6   Activate the Link tab.
7   Specify the field that you want to use to link the container and the subreport, and then click OK. The pointer changes to an arrow with a rectangular outline.
8   Click anywhere in the report to place the subreport.

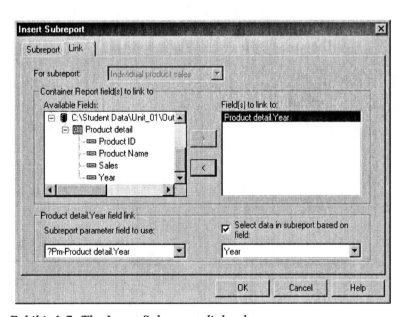

Exhibit 1-7: The Insert Subreport dialog box

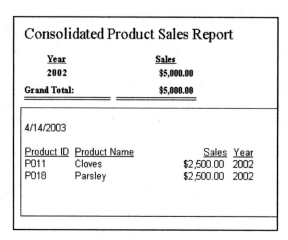

Consolidated Product Sales Report

Year	Sales
2002	$5,000.00
Grand Total:	$5,000.00

4/14/2003

Product ID	Product Name	Sales	Year
P011	Cloves	$2,500.00	2002
P018	Parsley	$2,500.00	2002

Exhibit 1-8: The Consolidated product sales report with a linked subreport

Consolidated Product Sales Report

Year	Sales
2001	$14,900.00
Grand Total:	$14,900.00

4/14/2003

Product ID	Product Name	Sales	Year
P001	Cinnamon ground	$4,000.00	2001
P010	Chervil	$2,000.00	2001
P012	Cumin	$1,200.00	2001
P017	Pepper	$5,000.00	2001
P019	Savoury	$1,500.00	2001
P020	Shallots	$1,200.00	2001

Exhibit 1-9: The Consolidated product sales report with a linked subreport

Do it!

B-2: Creating a linked subreport

Here's how	Here's why
⚠ *If you want to refresh report data, you'll need to set the database location for the report. However, that is not necessary to perform this activity.*	
1 Open Consolidated product sales report	The Vice President of Sales wants to view a report showing a year's sales summary as well as individual product sales for that year. To accomplish this, you'll create a linked subreport.
Activate the Design tab	
2 Open the Insert Subreport dialog box	(Choose Insert, Subreport.) Create a subreport is selected by default.
In the Report Name box, enter **Individual product sales**	
Click **Report Wizard**	To open the Standard Report Creation Wizard dialog box. The Data screen is active.
3 Expand **Create New Connection**	
Expand **Access/Excel (DAO)**	
Expand the Outlander Spices database	To list the tables in the database.
Add the Product detail table	Double-click Product detail.
4 Click **Next**	The Fields screen is activated. In the Available Fields list, under Product_detail, a list of fields appears.
Click [>>]	Fields to Display: ▲ ▼ ⬚ Product_detail.Product ID ⬚ Product_detail.Product Name ⬚ Product_detail.Sales ⬚ Product_detail.Year To add all of the fields.
Click **Finish**	To close the Standard Report Creation Wizard dialog box and return to the Insert Subreport dialog box.

5	Activate the Link tab	(To view the available fields.) You'll link this subreport to the container report.
	Under Product detail, select **Year**	You'll need to scroll down.
	Click [>]	To add the selected field to the Field(s) to link to list. Two new lists appear in the dialog box.
	Under Subreport parameter field to use list, verify that ?Pm-Product detail.Year is selected	The list displays the name of the field in the subreport that will be linked to the container report. A parameter field is created to link to the container report.
	Verify that Select data in subreport based on field is checked	This specifies that the data in the report will change based on the selected field, Year. The dialog box should look like Exhibit 1-7.
	Click **OK**	The pointer changes to an arrow with an outline.

6 In the Report Footer section, place the subreport as shown

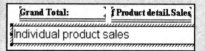

Deselect the subreport

| 7 | Preview the report | The report now looks like Exhibit 1-8. The container report shows the total sales for 2002, and the subreport displays the individual product sales for the same year. |
| 8 | Refresh the report data | |

> ○ Use current parameter values
> ○ Prompt for new parameter values
>
> Main report and Subreport data will all be refreshed.

		(Choose Report, Refresh Report Data.) The Refresh Report Data dialog box appears. Along with the parameter value options, a text message indicates that the subreport data will also be refreshed.
	Select **Prompt for new parameter values**	You'll display records based on a new parameter value.
	Click **OK**	The Enter Parameter Values dialog box appears, prompting for a value for Year.

9 In the Discrete Value box, enter **2001**	To display the sales report for 2001.
Click **OK**	Total sales for 2001 appear in the container report, with individual product sales for the year, as shown in Exhibit 1-9.
10 Save the report as **My consolidated product sales report**	If an Unable to Save Data With Report message appears, click Yes.
Close the report	

Unit summary: Complex reports

Topic A   In this unit, you learned how to create and use **parameter fields** to display report data based on a value entered by the user. Then, you learned how to apply an **edit mask** to a parameter field to accept formatted input. You also learned how to create and use a **pick list** to provide default values for a parameter field.

Topic B   Finally, you learned how to create **subreports**. You learned that the data in an **unlinked subreport** is not coordinated with that of its container report, whereas the data in a **linked subreport** changes based on what the user previews in the container report.

Independent practice activity

1 Open **Employee report** (from the current unit folder).

2 Create a parameter field, of the String data type, called **EmpID** with prompting text of your choice. Use this parameter field to get values for the field Employee ID.

3 Display data for the employee with Employee ID **E035** by using the saved data. Compare the data to Exhibit 1-10.

4 Save the report as **My employee report**.

5 Create a pick list containing all Employee ID values. Add the values to the list from the Employee ID field.

6 Display the data for the employee with Employee ID **E036**. Compare the data to Exhibit 1-11.

7 Update the report.

8 Create an on-demand linked subreport called **Employee leave report**. Add all the fields to the subreport from the database table Employee Leave Details in the Outlander Spices database. Link the container report and the subreport on the Employee ID field. Place the link to the subreport in the report footer.

9 Preview the subreport, and compare it to Exhibit 1-12.

10 Preview the container report.

11 Refresh the report to preview the details for the employee with Employee ID **E034**.

12 Click the subreport hyperlink to preview the subreport. Compare it to Exhibit 1-13.

13 Update and close the report.

Employee Report

Employee ID	Name	Address1	City	State
E035	James Owens	936 Fuhrman Rd.	Acampo	CA

Exhibit 1-10: The data for Employee ID E035, as displayed in Employee report

Employee Report

Employee ID	Name	Address1	City	State
E036	Robert Neil	23300 N Trethway Rd.	Acampo	CA

Exhibit 1-11: The data for Employee ID E036, as displayed in My employee report

Employee ID	Grade	Total Leave	Leave Availed
E036	G2	45	35

Exhibit 1-12: The data for Employee ID E036, as displayed in the subreport preview

Employee ID	Grade	Total Leave	Leave Availed
E034	G4	25	23

Exhibit 1-13: The data for Employee ID E034, as displayed in the subreport preview

Unit 2

Formatting complex reports

Unit time: 40 minutes

Complete this unit, and you'll know how to:

A Arrange field objects by adding, merging, and deleting report sections.

B Add hyperlinks and OLE objects.

Topic A: The Section Expert

Explanation

When you create a report, its objects are arranged in five default sections: Report Header, Page Header, Details, Report Footer, and Page Footer. To improve the report's readability, you can modify, delete, or merge the existing sections, or you can add sections by using the Section Expert.

Using the Section Expert

Choose Report, Section Expert to open the Section Expert dialog box. The Section Expert dialog box has two panes. The left pane contains a list of sections in the report, as well as buttons that permit you to insert, delete, and merge sections. The right pane contains two tabs. The Common tab displays the properties you can apply to the section selected in the left pane. The Color tab permits you to apply a background color to the selected section.

Adding sections

You add new sections by splitting the existing ones. For example, to arrange the field objects as shown in Exhibit 2-1, you would need to split the default Details section.

To add sections:

1   Choose Report, Section Expert to open the Section Expert dialog box.
2   From the Sections list, select a section.
3   Click Insert. The section will split into two new sections with "a" and "b" added at the end of the original section name.
4   Click OK to add these sections to the report. You can then arrange the data in these sections.

You can add more than one section to another section. Each time you add a new section of the same type, the other sections will be renamed accordingly. For example, in a report that already has sections named "Details a" and "Details b," if you add a section above Details b, the original Details b section will be renamed "Details c," and the new section will be named "Details b."

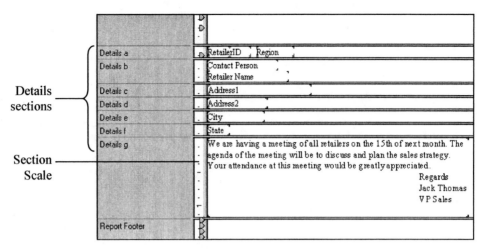

Exhibit 2-1: The fields arranged in sections for a form letter

```
R-OS-0001   West Coast
Shane Thomas
Ordeal Spices
70 Walton Ave Bronx

Manhattan
NY
We are having a meeting of all retailers on the 15th of next month. The
agenda of the meeting will be to discuss and plan the sales strategy.
Your attendance at this meeting would be greatly appreciated.
                                                Regards
                                                Jack Thomas
                                                VP Sales


R-OS-0002   East Coast
Jane Andrews
Spice World
210 New Falls Rd
Apt 224
Acampo
CA
We are having a meeting of all retailers on the 15th of next month. The
agenda of the meeting will be to discuss and plan the sales strategy.
Your attendance at this meeting would be greatly appreciated.
                                                Regards
                                                Jack Thomas
                                                VP Sales
```

Exhibit 2-2: The Retailer meeting letter after adding sections

Do it!

A-1:   Adding new sections

Here's how	Here's why
1 Open Retailer meeting letter	(From the current unit folder.) This is a Form Letter report. By using this report, you can print customized letters to be sent to several people.
Observe the report	The report contains retailers' names and addresses. It also contains the body of the letter in a text object, but the letter is not easy to read. You'll make this report more readable by adding new sections.
2 Activate the Design tab	
3 Choose **Report**, **Section Expert...**	To open the Section Expert dialog box.
From the Sections list, select **Details**	You'll add a second Details section below the current one.
Click **Insert**	The section is divided into two: Details a and Details b. The new section names appear in the list under the heading Details. Objects from the original Details section will appear in the Details a section, and the Details b section will be empty.
Click **OK**	
4 Click the text object containing the letter body, as shown	To select it.

Tell students that the entire text object must be in the Details b section before they release the mouse button.

Drag the text object from the Details a section to the Details b section, as shown	To move the body of the letter to a different section of the report.

	5 Open the Section Expert dialog box	Choose Report, Section Expert.
	6 From the Sections list, select **Details a**	You'll add a section below the Details a section.
	Click **Insert**	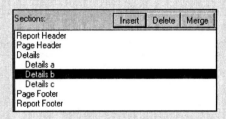
		A new section, Details c, appears.
Tell students that they might need to scroll down to see all three sections.	Click **OK**	There are now three details sections: Details a, Details b, and Details c. Because you added a section below Details a, it is added as "Details b." The previous Details b is renamed "Details c." The objects that were in the Details b section are now in the Details c section.
	7 Insert four more sections below Details b, as shown	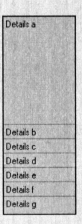
		(In the Section Expert dialog box, select Details b, click Insert four times, and click OK.) There are now seven Details sections, named "Details a" through "Details g."

	8 Point as shown	

To the border between the sections named Details b and Details c.

Drag the border down

To increase the size of the Details b section. The section scale should appear as shown.

Tell students to deselect the fields.

9   Move the Contact Person and Retailer Name fields from the Details a section to the Details b section

Place them as shown here.

10   Right-click the Details b heading

To display a shortcut menu.

     Choose **Fit Section**

The section is resized to fit only the fields.

11   Fit the Details a section, as shown

Tell students to right-click all the Details fields and choose Fit Section.

12   Arrange the rest of the fields

(As shown in Exhibit 2-1.) You might need to scroll to the right to see the rest of the fields.

     Deselect all fields

13   Preview the report

The meeting invitation is now formatted in sections, as shown in Exhibit 2-2.

14   Save the report as **My retailer meeting letter**

Modifying sections

Explanation

To modify report sections, use the Common tab of the Section Expert dialog box. This tab has several formatting options, as shown in Exhibit 2-3. You can specify a conditional formatting formula by clicking the conditional formula button next to an option. To modify a section, select the section from the Sections list. On the Common tab, check the option you want, and then click OK.

The following table describes some of the options on the Common tab:

Option	What it does
Suppress (No Drill-Down)	Hides a report section so that it's not printed or previewed.
Print at Bottom of Page	Forces the section contents to appear at the bottom of the page.
New Page Before	Inserts a page break before the section; for every record, the contents of this section will appear on a new page. (This option is available only for the Details, Group Header, and Group Footer sections.)
New Page After	Inserts a page break after the section; for every record, the contents of this section appear at the end of the page, with the next section appearing on a new page.
Suppress Blank Section	Hides a report section, but only if it's blank.

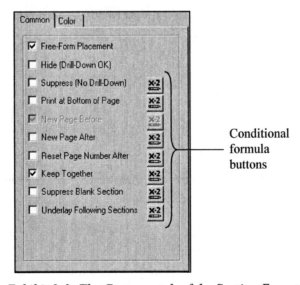

Exhibit 2-3: The Common tab of the Section Expert dialog box

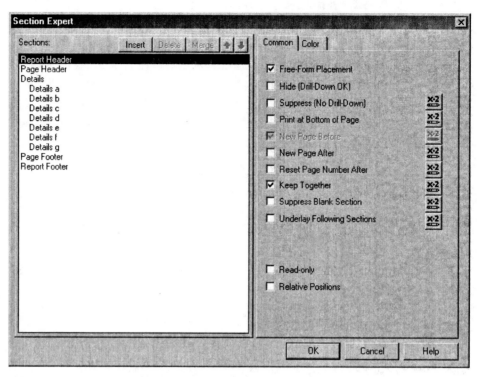

Exhibit 2-4: The Section Expert dialog box

Do it!

A-2: Suppressing a blank section

Here's how	Here's why
1 Select the blank area in the first record, as shown	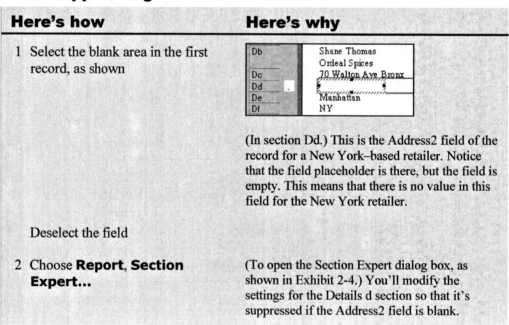
	(In section Dd.) This is the Address2 field of the record for a New York–based retailer. Notice that the field placeholder is there, but the field is empty. This means that there is no value in this field for the New York retailer.
Deselect the field	
2 Choose **Report, Section Expert...**	(To open the Section Expert dialog box, as shown in Exhibit 2-4.) You'll modify the settings for the Details d section so that it's suppressed if the Address2 field is blank.

3 Select **Details d**

   Check **Suppress Blank Section**   On the Common tab.

   Click the Suppress Blank Section conditional formula button, as shown

   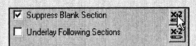

   To open the Formula Workshop – Format Formula Editor – Suppress Blank Section window. You'll apply a conditional formula to hide the section if it contains blank values for a field.

4 Expand **Report Fields**

   Under Report Fields, double-click **Retailer.Address2**   To add this field to the Formula text window.

   Enter **=""**   (An equal sign followed by two double quotes.) To specify that the section should be suppressed if the field Address2 is empty. The double quotes represent an empty text value.

   Click [Save and close]   To save the formula and close the Formula Editor window.

5 Click **OK**

   The Details d (Dd) section does not appear for this record.

6 Update the report

Merging sections

Explanation

When you print or preview reports with several sections, the fields for a given record might not all appear on the same page. To view these fields, you need to navigate through the report by using the bar in the Preview tab, as shown in Exhibit 2-5. In some cases, you can conserve space in a report by merging some of its sections. When you merge two sections, objects from both sections appear in a single section.

To merge sections, open the Section Expert, select a section, and click Merge. You can merge sections only if they are of the same type, such as Details. A section is always merged with the section immediately below it.

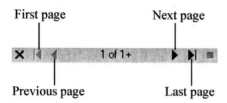

First page   Next page

1 of 1+

Previous page   Last page

Exhibit 2-5: The navigation bar in the Preview tab of the report

Details a	RetailerID Region
Details b	Contact Person Retailer Name Address1
Details c	Address2
Details d	City State We are having a meeting of all retailers on the 15th of next month. The agenda of the meeting will be to discuss and plan the sales strategy. Your attendance at this meeting would be greatly appreciated. Regards Jack Thomas V P Sales

Exhibit 2-6: The My retailer name report after sections are merged

Do it!

A-3:   **Merging report sections**

Here's how	**Here's why**
1 In the Preview tab, observe the navigation bar	(As shown in Exhibit 2-5.) The arrow buttons on both sides are used for navigating between the report pages.
2 Open the Section Expert dialog box	Choose Report, Section Expert.
Select **Details b**	You'll merge this section with the section below it.
Click **Merge**	The sections Details b and Details c are merged into one section in the Sections list, and the consecutive sections are renamed accordingly. A section is always merged with the section directly below it.
3 Click **OK**	To close the Section Expert dialog box.
4 Activate the Design tab	
Observe the report	
	The Details b and Details c sections have been merged into one section, and their contents now appear in a single section named "Details b."
Merge Details sections d, e, and f into one section	(In the Section Expert dialog box, select the Details d section, click Merge twice, and click OK.) The sections are merged into Details d, as shown in Exhibit 2-6. You are leaving Details c as a separate section so that the blank Address2 values will still be suppressed.
Deselect all fields	
Preview the report	
5 Click ▶	To view the next page of the report. The contact information (except for the retailer code and region) and letter text for the record appear together.
6 Update the report	

Tell students that they didn't merge the Details a section because they don't need it in this report. They will learn how to delete sections in the next activity.

Deleting sections

Explanation

You can delete only those sections that you have added; you cannot delete any of the five default sections. When you delete a section, its contents (the field objects) are also deleted from the report. To delete a section, open the Section Expert dialog box, select a section, and click Delete.

```
Shane Thomas
Ordeal Spices
70 Walton Ave Bronx
Manhattan
NY
We are having a meeting of all retailers on the 15th of next month. The
agenda of the meeting will be to discuss and plan the sales strategy.
Your attendance at this meeting would be greatly appreciated.
                                            Regards
                                            Jack Thomas
                                            V P Sales


Jane Andrews
Spice World
210 New Falls Rd
Apt 224
Acampo
CA
We are having a meeting of all retailers on the 15th of next month. The
agenda of the meeting will be to discuss and plan the sales strategy.
Your attendance at this meeting would be greatly appreciated.
                                            Regards
                                            Jack Thomas
                                            V P Sales
```

Exhibit 2-7: The My retailer name report after the Details a section is deleted

Do it!

A-4: Deleting a section

Here's how	Here's why
1 Click ⏮	R-OS-0001 West Coast Shane Thomas Ordeal Spices 70 Walton Ave Bronx Manhattan NY
	To view the first page of the report. The section containing the fields for retailer code and region is visible, along with the other sections for this record.
2 Open the Section Expert dialog box	
Select **Details a**	
Click **Delete**	Now, only Details a, b, and c appear in the sections list.
Click **OK**	Your report should look like Exhibit 2-7.
3 Update the report	

🔲 *Tell students that they will delete the Details a section because they don't need that information.*

Tell students that the space between the sections might differ depending on the placement of the fields in the earlier activity.

Displaying records on separate pages

Explanation

When printing a report, you might want to print each record on a separate page, especially if the report is a form letter. To do this, open the Section Expert, select a section, check New Page After (on the Common tab), and click OK.

Do it!

A-5: Displaying each record on a separate page

Here's how	Here's why
1 Scroll down to the end of the page	Notice that the records for Shane Thomas, Jane Andrews, and Julia Joseph appear on the same page. When these records are used as letters, you would want to print each record on a separate page.
Scroll up to the beginning of the page	
2 Open the Section Expert dialog box	
From the Sections list, select **Details**	
On the Common tab, check **New Page After**	To start a new page after each record in the details section.
Click **OK**	
3 Scroll down the page	Notice that only Shane Thomas's record appears on this page.
Click ▶	To move to the next page.
Observe the report	(Scroll up the page to view the record, if necessary.) The second record, for Jane Andrews, appears by itself on this page. The report now displays every record on a separate page.
4 Update and close the report	

Topic B: Objects

Explanation

In your report, you might want to display data that is saved in a format that Crystal Reports cannot understand. For example, you might have some data in a text file that you want to see when previewing the data. Or you might want to add a graphic from another program to the report. To display data from other applications, you can either create a *hyperlink* that connects to the file, or link or embed an OLE object.

Hyperlinks

You can create a hyperlink to refer to a local disk file, a field value, a Web site, or an e-mail address. To do so, you turn an existing report object into a hyperlink. Here's how:

1 Select a report object.
2 Choose Format, Hyperlink to open the Format Editor dialog box.
3 Select the type of hyperlink.
4 In the Hyperlink information box, enter the path of the hyperlink's target.
5 Click OK to create the hyperlink.

You can also create a hyperlink to another report, a process similar to inserting an on-demand subreport. To do this:

1 Verify that no objects are selected.
2 Choose Format, Hyperlink to open the Format Editor dialog box.
3 In the Crystal Report box, specify the file name and path of the report.
4 Click OK.

To access data by using a hyperlink, click the object on which you created the hyperlink.

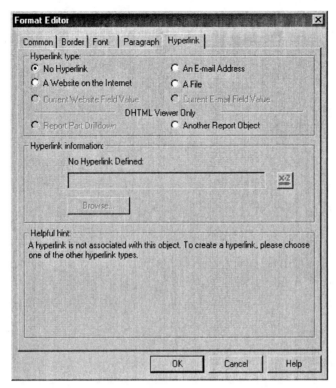

Exhibit 2-8: The Format Editor dialog box

Do it!

B-1:   Adding a hyperlink

Here's how	Here's why
1 Open Regional sales report	The Regional Manager wants to view a sales report for 2002 along with the sales target letter from the Vice President of Sales. Because the letter is in a text file, you'll add a hyperlink to that file.
Activate the Design tab	
2 Select the indicated text field	Click here to view the Sales target document for the Year 2002 Sale Amount
	On this report object, you'll create a hyperlink to the Sales target document.
Click	(The Insert Hyperlink button is on the Experts toolbar.) The Format Editor dialog box appears, as shown in Exhibit 2-8, with the Hyperlink tab activated.
Under Hyperlink type, select **A File**	To create a hyperlink to a local file on your computer. The File Name box becomes available.
Click **Browse**	The Open dialog box appears.
3 From the Files of type list, select **All Files**	
Select **Sales target document**	From the current unit folder.
Click **Open**	File Name: Sales target document.txt Browse...
	To return to the Format Editor dialog box. The name of the file is inserted in the File Name box.

4 Click **OK**   To create the hyperlink.

5 Deselect the fields

   Preview the report

6 Point as shown

> Click here to view
> the Sales target
> document for the
> Year 2002
>
> Sale Amount

The pointer changes to a hand, indicating that the text object is a hyperlink.

   Click the hyperlink   The text file, Sales target document, opens in Notepad.

   Close Notepad

7 Save the report as **My regional sales report**

OLE objects

Explanation

OLE stands for Object Linking and Embedding, a technology that permits you to add data from one application, called the *source*, to another application, called the *destination*. As the name suggests, by using OLE, you can insert linked or embedded objects. When you add a *linked OLE object* to a report, any changes made to the object in the source application will be reflected in the report. However, when you add an *embedded OLE object* to a report, any changes made to the object in the source application will *not* be reflected in the report.

You can create a new OLE object or add existing data as an OLE object. When creating a new OLE object, you can only embed it. You cannot link it because there is no source object. When you add an existing object, it can be linked or embedded.

To insert an OLE object based on an existing file:

1 Choose Insert, OLE Object to open the Insert Object dialog box.
2 Select Create from File, click Browse, select a file, and click Open.
3 Click OK. The pointer will change to an arrow with a rectangular outline.
4 Click where you want to place the object.

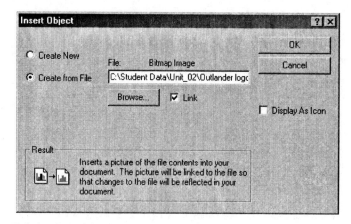

Exhibit 2-9: The Insert Object dialog box

Do it!

B-2: Adding a linked OLE object

Here's how	Here's why
1 Activate the Design tab	
2 Choose **Insert**, **OLE Object...**	To open the Insert Object dialog box. By default, Create New is selected. The Object Type list appears with the types of objects that you can insert.
Select **Create from File**	You'll insert an existing bitmap file as an OLE object. The File box appears in place of the Object Type list. A Browse button also appears.

3 Click **Browse**	To open the Browse dialog box.
Select **Outlander logo**	From the current unit folder.
Click **Open**	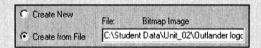
	The full path of the selected file is inserted in the File box. The file type (Bitmap Image) is indicated above the File box.
4 Check **Link**	To link the image to the original file. This will ensure that whenever you change the logo file, the changes will automatically be reflected in the report. The dialog box should look like Exhibit 2-9.
Click **OK**	
5 Click the Page Header section, as shown	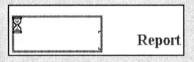
Observe the report	
	The Outlander Spices logo is added to the report.
6 Deselect all fields, and preview the report	
7 Select the Outlander Spices logo	
Double-click the Outlander Spices logo	The Paint window opens. It displays the bitmap image. You can modify the image here.
Close Paint	
8 Update and close the report	

⚠ *If a program other than Paint is set up as the default editor for bitmaps, that program will start instead.*

Tell students to click Yes if a dialog box appears.

Unit summary: Formatting complex reports

Topic A   In this unit, you learned how to add **sections** to organize report objects. You learned that you can use the **Section Expert** dialog box to **add**, **modify**, **merge**, and **delete** report sections.

Topic B   Finally, you learned how to create **hyperlinks** to refer to files in other applications. You also learned how to embed and link **OLE objects**.

Independent practice activity

1   Open **Market survey** (from the current unit folder.)

2   Modify the settings of the Page Header b section, so that the section does not appear when the report is previewed. (Hint: In the Section Expert dialog box, use the Suppress (No Drill-Down) option.)

3   Save the report as **My market survey**.

4   Delete the section Page Header c. Compare your report to Exhibit 2-10.

5   Insert a hyperlink on the text object **Click here to view the market survey document for 2002**. The hyperlink should point to the text file Market survey for 2002 (in the current unit folder.)

6   Using the hyperlink, open the text file Market survey for 2002. (Remember to deselect the text object first.)

7   Close the text file, and update the report.

8   Insert the bitmap image Market research seal as a linked OLE object, as show in Exhibit 2-11.

9   Deselect the OLE object.

10 Preview the report, and compare it to Exhibit 2-11.

11 Update and close the report.

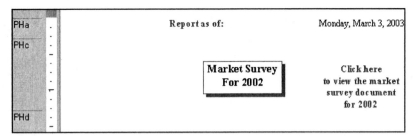

Exhibit 2-10: The My market survey report after the section Page Header c is deleted

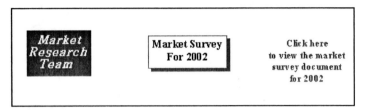

Exhibit 2-11: The My market survey report after the bitmap image is inserted

Unit 3

Advanced formulas and functions

Unit time: 70 minutes

Complete this unit, and you'll know how to:

A Create complex formulas by using variables, arrays, and ranges.

B Create formulas by using multiple functions and Evaluation Time functions.

C Specify conditions for repeating sets of steps in formulas by using For and While loops.

D Create and modify running totals.

Topic A: Variables

Explanation
In Crystal Reports, you can perform complex calculations by using formula components, such as variables, arrays, ranges, and loop constructs. You can also create complex formulas by combining available function types including Evaluation Time, summary, and string.

Variables in a formula

All the examples in this unit deal with creating formulas in Crystal syntax. Students can also use Basic syntax to write formulas in Crystal Reports; however, that syntax is not covered in this course.

You might need to create formulas that calculate values based on other calculated values. For example, let's say you have a report that displays production costs and total sales for each year, and you want it to display profit as a percentage of production cost. To do so, you first need to calculate the profit by subtracting production cost from total sales. You can then use this value to calculate the profit percentage.

To perform this type of calculation, you would store the first calculation's result so you could use it in the second calculation. You can do so by using a *variable*, which acts as a placeholder for a specific value. When a formula comes across a variable, the formula searches for and uses the value attached to that variable. You can store only one value at a time in a variable.

Each variable must have a name by which you can identify it. This name cannot be the same as any keyword, function, or operator in Crystal syntax. Variables must also be assigned a data type, such as number, string, or currency.

Variable declarations

To use a variable in a formula, you must first *declare* the variable—that is, you must specify its data type and name. The syntax for variable declaration is as follows:

```
<DataType><VariableName>;
```

The following table describes the syntax of some of the data types that Crystal Reports uses:

Data type	Description
NumberVar	Numeric variable.
CurrencyVar	Currency variable. (The values that you store in this type of variable are preceded by the currency symbol.)
StringVar	String (text) variable.
TimeVar	Variable that stores time values in an hours-minutes-seconds format, with "AM" or "PM" at the end.
DateVar	Variable that stores date values in a month-day-year format.

For example, here's how you would declare a numeric variable named X:

```
numberVar X;
```

To store a value in a variable, you use this syntax:

```
<VariableName> := <Value>;
```

For example, this is how you would assign the value 5 to variable X:

```
X := 5;
```

Variable scope

Scope defines the degree to which the variable can be used in other formulas. You specify a variable's scope when you define the variable. Crystal Reports offers three levels of scope: local, global, and shared.

Local variables can be used in only a single formula. To declare a local variable, use the following syntax:

```
Local numberVar X;
```

Global variables can be used throughout the main report. The value will be available to all formulas that declare it, but it will not be available within any subreports. To declare a global variable, you can use the following syntax:

```
Global numberVar X;
```

You can also declare a global variable by default by omitting the Global keyword.

Shared variables are available throughout the main report and all subreports. To declare a shared variable, you precede the declaration with the keyword "Shared."

Tell students that the formula's steps have been indented to make the formula easier to read, but this formatting is not necessary.

```
numberVar InvUnits := {Inventory stock.Quantity Purchased (In Packs)}-
{Inventory stock.Quantity Used (In Packs)};

if {Inventory items.Category} = "Flavoring Oils"
    then InvUnits * 25

else if {Inventory items.Category} = "Hot Sauces"
    then InvUnits * 50

else InvUnits * 75
```

Exhibit 3-1: A formula for calculating the cost of inventory on hand

Inventory Stock Report

Item No	Category	Quantity Purchased (In packs)	Quantity Used (In Packs)	Cost of inventory on hand
I001	Flavoring Oils	12000	10000	50,000.00
I002	Flavoring Oils	15000	12000	75,000.00
I003	Flavoring Oils	10000	9000	25,000.00
I004	Flavoring Oils	12000	10000	50,000.00
I005	Flavoring Oils	14000	12000	50,000.00
I006	Flavoring Oils	10000	8000	50,000.00
I008	Hot Sauces	9000	7000	100,000.00
I009	Hot Sauces	12000	11000	50,000.00
I010	Hot Sauces	11000	9800	60,000.00

Exhibit 3-2: The Inventory stock report after the Cost of inventory on hand field is added

Do it!

A-1: Declaring and using a variable in a formula

Here's how	Here's why
1 Open Inventory stock report	(From the current unit folder.) This report shows inventory purchased at the beginning of the year, as well as how much was used during the year. You'll declare a variable to store the inventory on hand at the end of the year. This value will be calculated by subtracting inventory used from inventory purchased.
Activate the Design tab	
2 Create a new formula named **Cost of inventory on hand**	(Choose View, Field Explorer; in the Field Explorer, select Formula Fields, and click the New button; in the Formula Name dialog box, specify the name for the formula and click Use Editor.) The Formula Workshop – Formula Editor – Cost of inventory on hand window appears.
3 Expand **Operators**	
Under Operators, expand **Variable Declarations**	Scroll down.
Double-click **NumberVar x :=y;**	(numberVar is the variable's data type.) A new variable is added to the Formula text window. No name has been specified for the variable yet.
Type **InvUnits**	This is the name of the variable.
4 Place the insertion point before the semi-colon, as shown	`numberVar InvUnits := ;`
5 Expand **Report Fields**	
Under Report Fields, double-click **Inventory stock.Quantity Purchased (In packs)**	To add this field to the Formula text window.
6 Type -	A minus sign.
Under Report Fields, double-click **Inventory stock.Quantity Used (In Packs)**	The formula will calculate the quantity of inventory stock on hand and store the result in the variable InvUnits. At this point, the first line of your formula should have the same information as the first two lines in Exhibit 3-1.

Tell students to maximize the Formula Workshop – Formula Editor – Cost of inventory on hand window, if necessary.

7   Place the insertion point after the semi-colon, as shown

`Inventory stock.Quantity Used (In Packs)};`

Press (⏎ ENTER)

8   Enter the rest of the formula

(As shown in Exhibit 3-1.) This formula uses an If construct to check a spice's category, and calculates the cost of inventory maintenance for the spice accordingly. The cost is calculated by multiplying the unit cost for that spice category by the variable InvUnits.

Click ▣ **x·2**

To check the formula for errors.

Click **OK**

If there were no errors. If there were errors, fix them and check the formula again.

Click ▣ **Close**

A message box prompting to save the changes appears.

Click **Yes**

To save the formula and close the Formula Editor window. Cost of inventory on hand is added under Formula Fields.

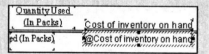

9   Place the formula field Cost of inventory on hand in the Details section, as shown

Format the formula field and heading with Times New Roman

Resize and position the formula field and heading as shown

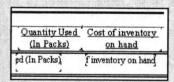

10   Preview the report

The cost of inventory on hand for each stock item appears, as shown in Exhibit 3-2.

11   Save the report as **My inventory stock report**

12   Close the report

Arrays

Explanation

You might need to use multiple values in a formula. For example, you might have six commission percentages that you use based on a salesperson's performance. You might also need to change the percentages at some point, meaning that you'd have to reflect these changes wherever the percentages are used in formulas. This process will be easier if you store the percentages in variables. However, because a variable can store only a single value, you'd need to use six variables to store the six percentage values, thus adding to the formula's complexity.

In this type of situation, you can use an array. An *array* is a kind of variable used to store multiple values of a single data type. To use an array in a formula, you need to declare the array. The syntax is as follows:

```
<DataType> array <ArrayName> := [Value1,Value2,Value3,....];
```

For example, here's the syntax for declaring an array named Y that stores four numeric values:

```
numberVar array Y := [15,20,25,30];
```

The values that are stored in the array—in this example, 15, 20, 25, and 30—are called the array *elements* and are referred to by a common name followed by a subscript. A *subscript* specifies the position of an element in an array. For example, in the array Y, the subscript for element 15 is 1, for element 20, it's 2, and so on. To use the value 15 in the formula, you can refer to it as Y[1]. The subscript of the first value of an array is always 1.

The subscript of the last element is called the *upper bound* of the array. It's the same as the number of elements in an array. To find out the value of the upper bound of an array, you can use a function called UBound. The syntax of the function is:

```
UBound (<ArrayName>);
```

This function returns the number of elements in an array as a numeric value, which can be useful when you're using looping constructs.

```
if {Direct Customers Sales.Sales} > 3000
    then {Direct Customers Sales.Sales} * DiscountPercent[1]

else if {Direct Customers Sales.Sales} >2500
    then {Direct Customers Sales.Sales} * DiscountPercent[2]

else if {Direct Customers Sales.Sales} > 2000
    then {Direct Customers Sales.Sales} * DiscountPercent[3]

else {Direct Customers Sales.Sales} * DiscountPercent[4]
```

Exhibit 3-3: The formula for calculating the discount amount for customers

Direct Customer Sales

Customer Code	City	Sales	Discount
C001	Aurora	1,500	75.00
C002	Amity	2,500	250.00
C003	Astoria	3,000	450.00
C004	Astoria	1,200	60.00
C005	Aumsville	2,700	405.00
C006	Portland	3,500	875.00
C007	Aumsville	3,200	800.00
C008	Portland	1,000	50.00
C009	Portland	1,500	75.00

Exhibit 3-4: The Direct customer sales report after the Discount field is added

Do it!

A-2: Using an array variable in a formula

Here's how	Here's why
1 Open Direct customer sales	You'll create a formula by using an array to calculate customer discounts. The array will store the various discount percentages. The advantage of using an array here is that instead of declaring four variables, you can declare a single array and refer to the array values by using subscripts.
Activate the Design tab	
2 Create a new formula named **Discount**	The Formula Workshop – Formula Editor – Discount window appears.
3 In the Formula text window, type the following code: `numberVar array DiscountPercent := [0.25,0.15,0.10,0.05];` 	To declare a numeric array named DiscountPercent. The array has four values.
4 Enter the rest of the formula	(As shown in Exhibit 3-3.) The formula uses the If construct to check the sales value. If it's greater than 3000, it's multiplied by DiscountPercent[1], which refers to the first array element, 0.25. In the same way, the formula calculates the discount for the rest of the sales amounts.
Check the formula; then save it and close the window	
5 Place the formula field Discount in the Details section, as shown	
Format the formula field and heading with Times New Roman	
Deselect the fields	
6 Preview the report	The discounts for each customer are indicated, as shown in Exhibit 3-4.
7 Save the report as **My direct customer sales**	
Close the report	

Remind students that they can double-click field names to add them to the formula.

The code for this formula can also be inserted from the file Discount.txt.

Range variables

Explanation
You use a range in a formula to check whether a value lies between specified limits. For example, in a sales report, you might want to find the names of salespersons whose total sales were between $10,000 and $20,000. A range has two end points: a lower limit and an upper limit. All the values that lie within these limits form part of the range.

Here's the syntax for declaring a range variable:

```
<DataType> range <RangeName> := <LowerLimit> to <UpperLimit>;
```

For example, to declare a range called "sales" with a data type of currency, you would use this syntax:

```
currencyVar range sales := 10000 to 20000;
```

To check whether a value lies within a range, you use the "in" keyword. For example, the following code will display the text between the quotes if the value of the salesvalue field lies within the sales range:

```
if Salestable.salesvalue in sales then "The sales value is ▶
        between 10000 to 20000"
```

```
numberVar range LowProfit := 0 to 0.24;

numberVar range NormalProfit:= 0.25 to 0.40;

numberVar CostProfitRatio := {Profit.Profit} / {Profit.Cost};

if  CostProfitRatio in LowProfit
    then "Below Average"

else if  CostProfitRatio in NormalProfit
      then "Normal"

else "Above Average"
```

Exhibit 3-5: A formula for displaying performance comments based on cost-profit ratio

Financial Analysis

Year	Cost	Profit	Business performance
1994	$40000	$10000	Normal
1995	$53500	$16500	Normal
1996	$105000	$45000	Above Average
1997	$85000	$15000	Below Average
1998	$180000	$70000	Normal
1999	$205000	$45000	Below Average
2000	$253000	$37000	Below Average
2001	$135000	$45000	Normal
2002	$225000	$75000	Normal

Exhibit 3-6: The Financial analysis report after the Business performance field is added

Do it!

A-3:   Using a range variable in a formula

Here's how	Here's why
1 Open Financial analysis	You'll create a formula that uses range variables to store ranges of cost-profit ratios. You'll then use these range values to evaluate a year's performance.
Activate the Design tab	
2 Create a new formula named **Business performance**	The Formula Workshop – Formula Editor – Business performance window appears.
3 In the Formula text window, type the following code:	

```
numberVar range LowProfit := 0 to 0.24;
```

	To declare a numeric range variable with 0 and 0.24 (or 24%) as the lower and upper limits.
4 Enter the rest of the formula	(As shown in Exhibit 3-5.) This formula first calculates the cost profit ratio for each year by dividing the profit amount by the cost amount. Next, the formula checks whether the ratio lies within either of two ranges. Then the formula displays a performance remark by using the If construct.
Check the formula, save it, and then close the window	
5 Place the formula field Business performance in the Details section, as shown	

The code for this formula can also be inserted from the file Business performance.txt.

Profit	Business performance
Profit	@Business performance

Format the formula field and heading with Times New Roman	
6 Preview the report	The remarks for each year appear, as shown in Exhibit 3-6.
7 Save the report as **My financial analysis**	

Remind students to deselect the field.

Topic B: Advanced functions

To help you create formulas, Crystal Reports provides several types of built-in functions, including String, Summary, Date/Time, and Evaluation Time. You can use these by themselves or in combination.

Using multiple functions in a formula

You can create a formula by using multiple functions to calculate a value. You can also combine multiple functions, field values, and text in a formula.

Combining functions, field values, and text

To combine different types of values in a formula, you use an ampersand (&), which is called the *concatenation* operator. It combines values from two different types of fields and returns a string type value. You can display this value in the formula field. Consider the following example:

```
stringVar DisplayValue;
DisplayValue := "The sales for the year 2002 are " & ▶
        Salestable.Sales
```

This code will combine a string and a sales value, and then store the resulting string in the DisplayValue variable.

Year	Cost	Profit	Business performance
1994	$40000	$10000	Normal
1995	$53500	$16500	Normal
1996	$105000	$45000	Above Average
1997	$85000	$15000	Below Average
1998	$180000	$70000	Normal
1999	$205000	$45000	Below Average
2000	$253000	$37000	Below Average
2001	$135000	$45000	Normal
2002	$225000	$75000	Normal

Financial Analysis

The average profit from 1994 to 2002 is $39,833.33

Exhibit 3-7: The Financial analysis report showing average profit for 1994 to 2002

Do it!

B-1: Creating a formula by using multiple functions

Here's how	Here's why
1 Activate the Design tab	The Vice President of Financial Services wants to view average profits for the last nine years.
2 Create a new formula named **Average profit**	The Formula Workshop – Formula Editor – Average profit window appears.
| 3 In the Formula text window, enter the formula shown | ```
"The average profit from 1994 to 2002 is $"
                   & Sum({Profit.Profit})/
                   Count({Profit.Year})
``` |
| | The formula uses the Sum and Count functions to calculate the average profit for nine years. The formula also combines text and calculations by using the concatenation operator (&). (Notice that Crystal syntax will ignore the line breaks in the code.) |

```
"The average profit from 1994 to 2002 is $"
& Sum({Profit.Profit})/
Count({Profit.Year})
```

Check the formula, save it, and close the window	
4 Place the formula field Average profit in the Report Footer section, as shown	
Format the formula field with Times New Roman	
Resize the formula field	To view the entire content.
5 Preview the report	It should look like Exhibit 3-7.
Update and close the report	

Remind students to deselect the field.
```

Evaluation Time functions

In the process of displaying records, a report passes through three stages:

1 Before the report reads the records from the database
2 While the report reads the records from the database
3 While the report prints the records read from the database

Each stage is called a *pass*. Crystal Reports evaluates the formulas in a report during any one of the passes, depending on the type of formula. Formulas that don't use any database fields are evaluated on the first pass; formulas that use database fields are evaluated during the second pass; and formulas that perform calculations on summary fields, such as subtotals, are evaluated during the third pass. When processing records, Crystal Reports uses *Evaluation Time functions* internally to decide which formula should be evaluated during which pass.

The following table describes the Evaluation Time functions:

Function	Description
BeforeReadingRecords	The formula is executed before the report reads the records from the database. You cannot use any database field in a formula in which you specify this function.
WhileReadingRecords	The formula is executed for each record as it's read from the database.
WhilePrintingRecords	The formula is executed when the report is displaying the records read from the database. This happens after the report has read all the records from the database.
EvaluateAfter (<FormulaName>)	This function takes a formula name as an argument. The formula in which you use it will be evaluated after the formula you specify as the EvaluateAfter argument.

In some situations, you might need to force a formula to be evaluated during a specific pass. To do this, you'll need to include an Evaluation Time function in the formula.

For example, let's say you have a function that calculates the customer discount and stores it in a variable named DiscountAmount. You also have a function that uses the DiscountAmount variable to calculate the final sales value. In the report, you want to display only the final sales value. Because you won't place the discount formula in the report, its formula won't be evaluated.

To calculate the final sales value, you'll need to use the EvaluateAfter function explicitly in the final amount formula by using the customer discount formula as the function's argument. If you do that, the customer discount formula will be evaluated first, producing the variable needed to calculate the final sales value.

```
numberVar array CommissionPercent := [0.12,0.10,0.05];
currencyVar Commission;

if {Saleperson.Sales Amount} > 5000 then
    Commission := {Saleperson.Sales Amount} * CommissionPercent[1]

else if {Saleperson.Sales Amount} > 2500 then
        Commission := {Saleperson.Sales Amount} * CommissionPercent[2]

else Commission := {Saleperson.Sales Amount} * CommissionPercent[3]
```

Exhibit 3-8: The formula for calculating salesperson commission

Do it!

B-2: Using the EvaluateAfter function

Here's how	Here's why
1 Open Salesperson remuneration	This report already has a formula named Commission that calculates each salesperson's commission. You'll create a formula that will calculate total remuneration, which is basic salary ($7000) plus commission.
View the formula for the Commission formula field	(In the Field Explorer, expand Formula Fields; select Commission; and click the Edit button.) The formula, shown in Exhibit 3-8, calculates commissions based on a sliding commission rate.
Close the Formula Editor window	
Activate the Design tab	The Commission formula has not been placed in the report because only the total remuneration needs to be shown. Next, you'll add a formula to calculate the total remuneration for each salesperson; this total is the sum of basic salary and commission.
2 Create a new formula named **Remuneration**	
In the Formula Editor window, enter the formula shown	```currencyVar Basic := 7000; currencyVar Commission; Basic + Commission```
	This formula stores the salesperson's basic salary in a variable named Basic. The formula then declares the variable Commission but doesn't specify a value because the variable should refer to the value of the variable with the same name in the Commission formula. The formula then calculates the sum of the basic salary and the commission.

3 Check the formula, save it, and
   then close the window

4 Place the Remuneration formula
   in the Details section, as shown

Sales Amount	Remuneration
Sales Amount	Remuneration

   Format the Remuneration formula
   field and heading with Times New
   Roman

   Resize the formula field to view
   the entire formula

Remind students to deselect the field.

5 Preview the report

Remuneration
$7,000.00
$7,000.00
$7,000.00
$7,000.00
$7,000.00
$7,000.00
$7,000.00
$7,000.00

   The Remuneration formula field shows all the
   values as $7000.00, which is the value of each
   salesperson's basic salary. This is because the
   Commission variable has not been initialized in
   this formula, nor has the Commission formula
   been evaluated.

6 In the Field Explorer, select
   Remuneration

   (If necessary.) To calculate the correct
   remuneration value, you'll use the EvaluateAfter
   function to force the Commission formula to be
   evaluated before the Remuneration formula.

   Click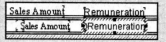

   To open the Formula Workshop – Formula
   Editor – Remuneration window.

7 Place the insertion point in the
   indicated position

```
currencyVar Basic := 7000;
currencyVar Commission;

Basic + Commission
```

   You'll enter code above the variable
   declarations.

   Type the following code:

   ```
   EvaluateAfter({@Commission});
   ```

   To evaluate the Commission formula before the
   Remuneration formula is evaluated.

   Press [↵ ENTER]

8 Observe the formula

```
EvaluateAfter({@Commission});
CurrencyVar Basic := 7000;
CurrencyVar Commission;

Basic + Commission
```

The formula should look like this.

9 Check the formula, save it, and then close the window

10 Observe the Remuneration formula field

Remuneration
$7,075.00
$7,720.00
$7,500.00
$7,400.00
$7,100.00
$7,075.00
$7,100.00
$7,125.00

The total remuneration as a sum of basic salary and commission now appears in the formula. This is because the Commission formula is now forced to execute before the Remuneration formula.

11 Save the report as **My salesperson remuneration**

Close the report

Topic C: Constructs

Explanation

You use *constructs* in a formula to specify which set of steps should be executed and when. Constructs—also called *control structures*—evaluate a condition to decide whether to execute a set of steps. This process is called *looping*. The most common constructs are If-then-else, For, and While.

For constructs

You use the *For* construct when you want to execute a set of steps a certain number of times. Use this construct when you know the exact number of times the steps should execute. The syntax is as follows:

```
for <VariableName> := <InitialValue> to <FinalValue> ▶
    step <Value> do
(
steps
);
```

A For construct uses a *counter variable* as a looping counter. The value of this variable at any point in time determines whether the steps inside the parentheses will execute. The construct executes in three steps:

1   It first sets the value of the counter variable to the initial value. This process is called *initialization*.

2   It then checks whether the value of the counter variable lies between the initial value and the final value, inclusively. This is called a *condition test*. If the condition evaluates to yes, then the loop condition is true. If the condition evaluates to no, then the loop condition is false. If the condition is true, the construct executes the steps between the parentheses following the do keyword. If not, the loop terminates, and the steps after the construct are executed.

3   It then increases the counter variable by the value specified after the step keyword. This value is called an *increment*.

Steps 2 and 3 are repeated until the condition test becomes false—that is, when the value of the counter variable exceeds the final value.

In the For construct syntax, the initialization, condition test, and increment steps are placed as a single step in the formula.

For example:

```
numberVar i;
numberVar j;
for i := 1 to 5 step 1 do
(
j:= j + 2
);
```

In this example, the formula begins by declaring variables i and j. The loop initializes the value of i to one (1). The loop will then check whether the value of i lies between 1 and 5. If yes, then it will increment j by two. Then the loop will increment the value of i by one, as specified after the step keyword, and then check the condition again. The steps in this For loop will be executed five times.

The For construct can terminate in two ways:

- If the condition in the loop becomes false
- If an exit for step is specified in the loop

```
numberVar RisePercent := 0.20;

numberVar CurrentYrProfit := 25000;

numberVar Ctr;

numberVar RiseInProfit;

stringVar FinalString := "The estimated profit for the next three years is: ";

for Ctr := 1 to 3 step 1 do
(
    RiseInProfit := CurrentYrProfit * RisePercent;
    CurrentYrProfit := CurrentYrProfit + RiseInProfit;
    FinalString := FinalString & "      " & CurrentYrProfit;
);

FinalString
```

Exhibit 3-9: The formula for estimating and displaying profit for the next three years

Do it!

C-1: Using a For construct

Here's how	Here's why
1 Open Estimated profit calculation	You'll insert a formula in this report to calculate the estimated profit for the next three years based on a profit rise percentage. You'll use the For construct to calculate the estimated profit.
Activate the Design tab	
2 Create a new formula named **Estimated profit**	The Formula Workshop – Formula Editor – Estimated profit window appears.
3 In the Formula text window, enter the formula	As shown in Exhibit 3-9.
Observe the first two variable declarations	RisePercent and CurrentYrProfit set values for the projected percentage of profit increase and the profits for the current year.
Observe the Ctr variable	This will be the counter in the For construct.
Observe the next two variable declarations	The RiseInProfit variable will be used to calculate the projected rise in profit. The FinalString variable will contain the message that the function will ultimately return.
4 Observe the For construct	The Ctr variable is initialized to 1, the steps are executed, then Ctr is increased by the step value (1). The construct will execute exactly three times.
	The steps within the construct calculate each year's projected profit, and then combine the FinalString message with some space and the profit value. After the steps execute three times, the FinalString includes all three projected profit values.
Observe the last step in the formula	This line returns the FinalString value.
Check the formula, save it, and then close the Formula Editor window	

The code for this formula can also be inserted from the file Estimated profit.txt.

5   Place the Estimated profit field in
    the Report Footer section, as
    shown

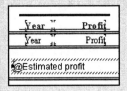

Be sure to put the field below the year text
labels.

Format the Estimated profit field
with Times New Roman

Resize the formula field as shown

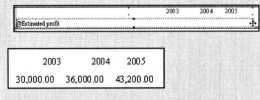

*Remind students to
deselect the field.*

6   Preview the report

	2003	2004	2005
	30,000.00	36,000.00	43,200.00

To view the estimated profits for all years.

*Ask students if they can
think of other ways to
achieve the same result in
a report.*

7   Save the report as **My
    estimated profit
    calculation**

    Close the report

While constructs

Explanation

You use a *While* construct in situations when you don't know the number of times the loop should execute. This construct executes a set of steps repeatedly while a specified condition is true. In the While construct (unlike in a For construct), the steps for initialization, condition test, and increment are placed in separate steps. The syntax is as follows:

```
while <condition> do
(
steps
increment step
);
```

It's important to put an increment step within the loop. If you don't, the loop will never end because the value of the counter variable will never change.

A While construct can terminate in two ways:

- If the condition in the construct becomes false

- If an `exit while` step is specified in the loop

```
stringVar Name := {Direct Customers.Customer Name};
numberVar i:= 1;
numberVar Strlen := length (Name);
NumberVar Result:= -1;

while i <= Strlen and Result= -1 do
(
    stringVar Position:= mid (Name, i, 1);
    if  Position =" " then
        Result:= i;
    i:= i + 1;
);
stringvar Lastname:= mid (Name, Result+1, (Strlen-Result));
Lastname
```

Exhibit 3-10: The formula for retrieving the last names of customers

Customer Records

Customer Name	Last name
Mark Peterson	Peterson
Rita Greg	Greg
Anna Morris	Morris
Monica Dukes	Dukes
Nikki Cleary	Cleary
Annie Philips	Philips
Paul Anderson	Anderson
Jesse Bennet	Bennet
Jamie Morrison	Morrison

Exhibit 3-11: The Customer records report after the Last name field is added

Do it!

C-2:   Using a While construct

Here's how	Here's why
1 Open Customer records	In this report, you'll insert a formula that uses a While construct to retrieve the last names of customers.
Activate the Design tab	
2 Create a new formula named **Last name**	
3 In the Formula text window, enter the formula	As shown in Exhibit 3-10.
4 Observe the variable declarations	The first variable will store the full names retrieved from the database table.
	The variable i will be the counter for the While construct.
	The Strlen variable will use the LEN function to calculate the number of characters in the Name variable.
	The Result variable is specified as -1. This value will be changed when the loop encounters a space, enabling the code to exit the loop.
5 Observe the While construct	The loop will be executed as long as the counter value is less than or equal to the number of characters in the Strlen variable (the number of characters in the name), and as long as the value of the Result variable is -1.
	The variable Position uses the MID function to retrieve each character in the Name variable.
	The If construct checks whether the character retrieved by the Position variable is a space. If it is, the counter value gets stored in the Result variable and the loop exits.
	If the condition returns false, the counter is incremented by 1 and the loop continues, checking the next character in the name.

The code for this formula can also be inserted from the file Last name.txt.

6 Observe the last line of the formula

The Lastname variable uses the MID function to retrieve the position of the first character to extract and the number of characters to be extracted from the text string. This has the result of returning the last name.

7 Check the formula, save it, and then close the window

8 Place the Last name field in the Details section, as shown

Customer Name	Last name
Customer Name	@Last name

Format the Last name formula field and heading with Times New Roman

Deselect the fields

Point out that while this report might not be realistic, it demonstrates the use of the While construct to extract parts of a text field.

9 Preview the report

The last names of customers appear, as shown in Exhibit 3-11.

Save the report as
My customer records

Close the report

Topic D: Running totals

Explanation

When creating a report, you might need to calculate an incremental total for a specific field on each record. You perform this specific function by using running totals. You can identify a running total field by the # sign at the beginning of the running total field's name.

Create a running total

To create a running total field:

1   In the Field Explorer, select Running Total Fields.

2   Click the New button to open the Create Running Total Field dialog box, as shown in Exhibit 3-12.

3   Complete the dialog box and click OK. The field is then listed in the Field Explorer, under Running Total Fields.

4   Select the field you just created, and drag it onto the report.

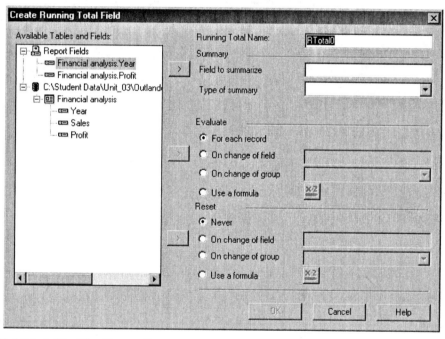

Exhibit 3-12: The Create Running Total Field dialog box

Running total

Year	Profit	Total profit
1990	15,000	15,000.00
1991	12,000	27,000.00
1992	14,000	41,000.00
1993	10,000	51,000.00
1994	15,000	66,000.00
1995	17,000	83,000.00
1996	18,000	101,000.00
1997	16,000	117,000.00
1998	20,000	137,000.00
1999	21,000	158,000.00
2000	25,000	183,000.00

Exhibit 3-13: The Running total report created at the end of the activity

Do it!

D-1: Creating a running total

Here's how	Here's why
1 Open Running total report	
Activate the Design tab	
2 From the Field Explorer, select **Running Total Fields**	You'll create a running total for the profit field.
3 Click ⊞	(The New button is in the toolbar.) To display the Create Running Total Field dialog box, as shown in Exhibit 3-12.
4 Edit the Running Total Name box to read **Total profit**	To name the running total field.
5 From the Available Tables and Fields list, select **Financial analysis.Profit**, as shown	⊟ 🔲 Report Fields ▭ Financial analysis.Year ▭ Financial analysis.Profit
Click ⟩	To add the Financial analysis.Profit field to the Field to summarize box.
In the Type of summary list, verify that sum is selected	
Under Evaluate, verify that For each record is selected	You'll display a running total for every field.
Click **OK**	(To apply the changes and close the Create Running Total Field dialog box.) Total profit is added under Running Total Fields in the Field Explorer.
6 Place the Total profit field in the Details section, as shown	Profit Total profit Profit Total profit
Format the Total profit field and heading with Times New Roman	
Resize the Total profit field to view all its contents	
7 Preview the report	The report will look like the one shown in Exhibit 3-13.
8 Save the report as **My running total report**	

Modify a running total

Explanation

You modify a running total field by using the Edit Running Total Field dialog box. This dialog box appears when you select the running total and click the Edit button in the Field Explorer dialog box. Another method of displaying this dialog box is by right-clicking the running total field and choosing Edit Running Total from the shortcut menu.

Running total

Year	Profit	Total profit
1990	15,000	15,000.00
1991	12,000	13,500.00
1992	14,000	13,666.67
1993	10,000	12,750.00
1994	15,000	13,200.00
1995	17,000	13,833.33
1996	18,000	14,428.57
1997	16,000	14,625.00
1998	20,000	15,222.22
1999	21,000	15,800.00
2000	25,000	16,636.36

Exhibit 3-14: The modified Running total report

Do it!

D-2: Modifying a running total

Here's how	Here's why
1 Activate the Design tab	You'll modify the running total field to display the average profit.
2 Verify that Total profit is selected in the Field Explorer	
Click [pencil icon]	(The Edit button is in the toolbar.) To display the Edit Running Total Field dialog box.
3 From the Type of summary list, select **average**	You'll modify the Total profit field to display the average profit for each record.
4 Click **OK**	To apply the changes and close the Edit Running Total Field dialog box.
5 Preview the report	The report will look like the one shown in Exhibit 3-14.
6 Observe the report	The Total profit field displays the average profit up to that record.
7 Update and close the report	

Unit summary: Advanced formulas and functions

Topic A

In this unit, you learned that you can use a **variable** to store a value. Then, you learned that you can use an **array** to store multiple values of the same type. You also learned how to use a **range variable** to test whether a value lies between an upper and a lower limit.

Topic B

Next, you learned how to create formulas by using multiple functions. You learned how to use the **concatenation operator** to combine different types of values. You also learned how to use **Evaluation Time functions** to specify when a formula should be evaluated.

Topic C

Then, you learned how to use **looping constructs**. You learned that you can use the **For construct** to execute a set of steps a certain number of times, and you can use the **While construct** to execute a set of steps while a certain condition is true.

Topic D

Finally, you learned about **running totals**. You learned that you can **create a running total** by using the Create Running Total Field dialog box. You also learned how to **modify a running total** by using the Edit Running Total Field dialog box.

Independent practice activity

1 Open **Shipping costs**.

2 Create a new formula called **Shipping costs per sale**. The formula should calculate total shipping cost for each sale performed. The total shipping cost is calculated as the total number of shipping days multiplied by the shipping cost per day. The number of shipping days is calculated as Delivery date minus (-) Shipping date. Store the number of shipping days in a numeric variable. The shipping costs are $50 per day. (Hint: The completed code for this formula is in the file Shipping.txt.)

3 Place the formula after the Delivery date field.

4 Preview the report and compare it to Exhibit 3-15.

5 Save the report as **My shipping costs**.

6 Close the report.

7 Which Evaluation Time function would you use to perform a formula calculation before the report reads the records to display from the database?

BeforeReadingRecords

8 Which construct would you use to execute a set of steps a known number of times?

The For construct

9 Open **Estimated profit**.

10 Create a new formula called **Estimated profit**. Calculate the profit for the next five years starting from 2003. Calculate the profit for each year by increasing the previous year's profit by 25%. The profit for 2001 should be taken as the current year's profit. (The completed code for this is in the file Practice profit.txt.)

11 Preview the report and compare it to Exhibit 3-16.

12 Save the report as **My estimated profit**.

13 For the year field, insert a running total called **Year count** that displays the year count on each record. (Hint: From the Type of summary list, select count.) Format the field to match other fields in the report, and compare it to Exhibit 3-17.

14 Update and close the report.

Sale ID	Shipping date	Delivery date	Shipping costs per sale
S 001	08/23/2002	08/30/2002	350.00
S 003	08/30/2002	09/05/2002	300.00
S 002	08/25/2002	09/01/2002	350.00
S 003	09/01/2002	09/07/2002	300.00
S 005	09/07/2002	09/10/2002	150.00
S 006	09/08/2002	09/12/2002	200.00
S 007	09/08/2002	09/14/2002	300.00
S 008	09/08/2002	09/17/2002	450.00
S 009	09/10/2002	09/22/2002	600.00
S 010	09/19/2002	09/25/2002	300.00
S 012	09/12/2002	09/14/2002	100.00
S 011	09/10/2002	09/15/2002	250.00
S 013	09/14/2002	09/17/2002	150.00
S 014	10/08/2002	10/10/2002	100.00
S 015	10/08/2002	10/10/2002	100.00
S 016	10/15/2002	10/17/2002	100.00
S 017	10/08/2002	10/12/2002	200.00
S 018	11/08/2002	11/15/2002	350.00
S 019	09/25/2002	09/27/2002	100.00
S 020	12/08/2002	12/10/2002	100.00

Exhibit 3-15: The report after step 4 of the Independent Practice Activity

Estimated Profit calculation

Year	Profit
1990	25,000
1991	28,000
1992	18,000
1993	16,000
1994	22,000
1995	24,000
1996	20,000
1997	26,000
1998	23,000
1999	25,000
2000	22,000
2001	24,000

	2003	2004	2005	2006	2007
The Estimated Profit for the next five years is:	30,000.00	37,500.00	46,875.00	58,593.75	73,242.19

Exhibit 3-16: The report after step 10 of the Independent Practice Activity

Estimated Profit calculation								
Year	**Profit**	**Year count**						
1990	25,000	1						
1991	28,000	2						
1992	18,000	3						
1993	16,000	4						
1994	22,000	5						
1995	24,000	6						
1996	20,000	7						
1997	26,000	8						
1998	23,000	9						
1999	25,000	10						
2000	22,000	11						
2001	24,000	12						
				2003	2004	2005	2006	2007
The Estimated Profit for the next five years is:				30,000.00	37,500.00	46,875.00	58,593.75	73,242.19

Exhibit 3-17: The report after step 13 of the Independent Practice Activity

Unit 4

Advanced data access techniques

Unit time: 120 minutes

Complete this unit, and you'll know how to:

A Use dictionaries to create and modify views of data relevant to different users.

B Access data from different types of databases by using ODBC.

C Use Crystal SQL Designer to create SQL queries, and use queries to create reports.

D Create, modify, and delete report alerts.

Topic A: Dictionaries

Explanation

You can use dictionaries to organize data so that it's easily accessible. A *dictionary* is a data view that you use to provide only relevant data to the user. You can add data, formulas, and graphics from several databases to a dictionary.

Dictionaries do not prevent users from accessing data directly. However, dictionaries can make it easier to organize and present data by providing the following:

- A single view of all the data necessary to create company reports
- Options for renaming tables and fields, as well as for organizing data to make it easier to understand
- Options for creating complex formulas that a user can employ

Creating dictionaries

To create a dictionary, use the Crystal Dictionaries tool. To do this:

1 Choose Start, Programs, Crystal Data Compatibility Tools, Crystal Dictionaries to open the Crystal Dictionaries window.

2 Click New to open the Crystal Dictionary window (also called the Crystal Dictionary Expert).

3 Create the dictionary; then click Save to save it. The dictionary is saved with a .dc5 extension.

The Crystal Dictionary Expert

The Crystal Dictionary Expert has five tabs: Tables, Links, View, Graphic, and Sample. You can use these tabs to guide you through the process of creating a dictionary. When you open the Crystal Dictionary Expert, it appears with all the tabs except for Links. The tabs are described in the following table:

Tab	Use this tab to...
Tables	Add tables to a dictionary. (You can add tables from different databases.)
Links	Show the links between the selected tables. (This tab is available only if multiple tables are selected.)
View	Add table fields, change the names of fields and tables in a dictionary (by using the Alias button), and add formulas to a dictionary (by using the New Formula button.)
Graphic	Add picture files to a dictionary.
Sample Data	Add sample data from the tables to the dictionary. (The data will be saved along with the dictionary.)

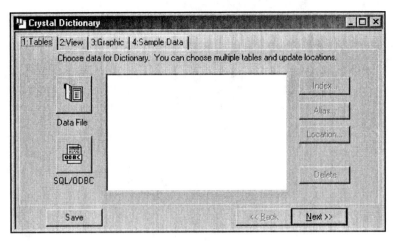

Exhibit 4-1: The Crystal Dictionary window

Do it!

A-1: Creating a dictionary

Here's how	Here's why
1 Choose **Start**, **Programs**, **Crystal Data Compatibility Tools**, **Crystal Dictionaries**	To display the Crystal Dictionaries window. You'll create a new dictionary of customer order data for 2002. The Production department needs this information.
2 Click **New**	(On the toolbar.) To open the Crystal Dictionary window, also called the Crystal Dictionary Expert, as shown in Exhibit 4-1. The 1:Tables tab is activated.
3 Click [icon]	To open the Choose Database File dialog box.
4 From the File Name list, select **Customers – Order.mdb**	(From the current unit folder.) You'll create a dictionary from this database.
Click **Add**	

TIPS ✓ *Tell students that they can also choose File, New Dictionary to open the Crystal Dictionary window.*

	The Select Tables dialog box appears. Three tables are listed: Customers, Order Details, and Products.
5 Click **Select All**	
Click **OK**	To add all three tables to the dictionary and return to the Choose Database File dialog box.
6 Click **Done**	To close the Choose Database File dialog box.
7 Click **Next**	To activate the 2:Links tab. Here you can view and modify table relationships.

8 Observe the table relationships

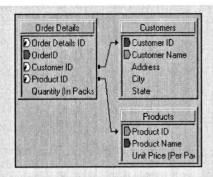

There are three database tables in this relationship. The Order Details table is linked to the Customers table by the key Customer ID, and to the Products table by the key Product ID.

9 Click **Next**

To activate the 3:View tab.

10 From the Tables & fields from database list, select **Order Details**, as shown

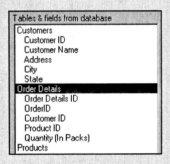

Click **Add**

To add the selected table to the dictionary. The table and its field names are added to the Headings & fields in View list.

11 In the Headings & fields in View list, verify that Order Details is selected

Under the second list, click **Alias**, as shown

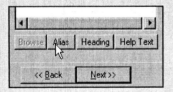

To open the Set Table Alias dialog box.

Edit the Enter a new table alias box to read **Customer-Order**

Click **OK**

In the Headings & fields in View list, notice that the name of the table has changed. The table will be identified by this name in the dictionary.

12 From the first list, under Products, select **Unit Price (Per Pack)**

You'll add this field to the dictionary.

From the second list, select **Quantity (In Packs)**

When you add a field, it will be inserted below the selected field in this list.

Click **Add**

To add the Unit Price (Per Pack) field below the Quantity (In Packs) field in the dictionary.

13 Under the first list, click **New Formula**

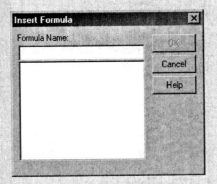

To open the Insert Formula dialog box. You'll create a new formula and add it to the dictionary.

In the Formula Name box, enter **Sales Value**

Click **OK**

To open the Edit Formula: @Sales Value dialog box.

14 Enter the following formula:

```
{Order Details.Quantity (In Packs)}*
    {Products.Unit Price (Per Pack)}
```

Click **Accept**

To return to the Crystal Dictionary Expert. In the Tables & fields from database list, Sales Value appears under Formulas.

15 Add the formula Sales Value to the Headings & fields in View list

From the Tables & fields from database list, select Sales Value, and then click Add.

16	Activate the 5:Sample Data tab	You'll add sample data from the table to the dictionary.
	From the Headings & fields in View list, select **Order Details ID**	
	Click **Collect**	To add the data from the field to the Browsed data list. It will be saved with the dictionary.
	Add the data for the remaining fields, except the Sales Value formula, to the Browsed data list	The Sales Value formula will be evaluated when you use this dictionary to create the report.
17	Click **Save**	To open the File Save As dialog box.
	Select the current unit folder	If necessary.
	Edit the File name box to read **My customer order**	
	Click **OK**	To save the dictionary with a .dc5 extension.
18	Choose **File, Exit**	To close Crystal Dictionaries.

TIPS
✔ *Tell students that they can also use the Shift and arrow keys to select multiple fields from the list.*

Using dictionaries

Explanation
When you use a dictionary to create a report, you can use only the data available through the dictionary. You cannot use data from any other source, such as an Access database. To create a report based on a dictionary:

1 Open the Crystal Reports Gallery. Under Choose a Wizard, Standard is selected. Click OK.

2 In the Report Wizard, double-click Dictionary/Infoview to display the Open dialog box.

3 Select a dictionary file.

4 Add all the tables in the dictionary to the Selected Tables list.

5 Follow the Report Wizard steps to create the report.

If the dictionary contains any pictures, a new tree named Dictionary Graphics will be added to the Field Explorer. You can select and add these pictures to the report.

				powered by **crystal**		
Report Description:						
10	O-OS-002	C007	P003	16	$22.00	$ 352.00
33	O-OS-012	C001	P004	16	$23.00	$ 368.00
11	O-OS-004	C009	P005	17	$24.00	$ 408.00
14	O-OS-005	C003	P005	25	$24.00	$ 600.00
15	O-OS-006	C006	P006	22	$27.00	$ 594.00
16	O-OS-007	C008	P006	25	$27.00	$ 675.00
17	O-OS-008	C008	P006	27	$27.00	$ 729.00
1	O-OS-001	C002	P007	15	$28.00	$ 420.00
23	O-OS-018	C009	P007	25	$28.00	$ 700.00
12	O-OS-003	C001	P008	18	$21.00	$ 378.00

Exhibit 4-2: The report created by using the My customer order dictionary

Do it!

A-2:   Using a dictionary to create a report

Here's how	Here's why
1 Activate the Crystal Reports window	If necessary.
2 Open the Crystal Reports Gallery	(Click the New button.) Under Choose a Wizard, Standard is selected.
Click **OK**	To open the Standard Report Creation Wizard dialog box.
3 Expand **Create New Connection**	
Double-click **Dictionary/Infoview**	To display the Open dialog box.
Select **My customer order**	From the current unit folder.
Click **Open**	
4 Verify that Customer-Order is selected, as shown	
Add Customer-Order to the Selected Tables list	
5 Click **Next**	
Add all the dictionary fields to the Fields to Display list	Click Add All.
6 Click **Next** three times	To activate the Template screen.
From the Available Templates list, select **Block (Blue)**	
7 Click **Finish**	To create the report.
Arrange the report fields	The report should look like the one shown in Exhibit 4-2. The Sales Value field shows the total sales for each order, which is calculated by the formula stored in the dictionary.
8 Save the report as **My customer order report**	
9 Close the report	

Modifying a dictionary

Explanation

To modify a dictionary:

1   Open the Crystal Dictionaries window.
2   Add or delete fields from the dictionary.
3   Choose Refresh, Report Data to refresh the data in the report to reflect the changes made in the report's dictionary.

Do it!

A-3:   Modifying a dictionary

Here's how	Here's why
1 Close Crystal Reports	(To refresh the data in the report.) Choose File, Exit.
2 Open the Crystal Dictionaries window	Choose Start, Programs, Crystal Data Compatibility Tools, Crystal Dictionaries.
3 Click **Open**	To display the File Open dialog box.
4 Select **My customer order.dc5**	From the current unit folder.
Click **OK**	To open the Crystal Dictionary: MY CUSTOMER ORDER window. The 1:Tables tab is activated.
5 Click the **3:View** tab	
Under Headings & fields in View list, select **Customer ID**	You'll delete this field from the dictionary.
Click **Remove**	To remove the Customer ID field from the Headings & fields in View list.
Click **Save**	To save the changes.
6 Choose **File, Close**	To close the dictionary.
Close the Crystal Dictionaries window	Choose File, Exit.

Tell students to maximize the Crystal Dictionaries window, if necessary.

Tell students that if Crystal Decisions Registration Wizard appears, click Register Later.

7	Start Crystal Reports	Choose Start, Programs, Crystal Reports 9.
8	Open My customer order report	From the current unit folder.
	Observe the report	The report contains the field Customer ID. This field will not be shown after you refresh the report data. This is because this field has been removed from the My customer order dictionary that is used to create the report.
9	Choose **Report, Refresh Report Data**	(A message box appears.) You'll refresh the report to reflect the changes made in the dictionary.
	Click **OK**	A message box, prompting you to fix the report, appears.
	Click **OK**	The Map Fields dialog box appears.
	Click **OK**	(To close the Map Fields dialog box.) A message box, telling you that the database is up-to-date, appears.
	Click **OK**	
10	Observe the report	The data in the report is updated to reflect the changes made in the dictionary.
11	Update and close the report	

Topic B: ODBC data sources

Explanation

ODBC stands for *Open Database Connectivity*. This technology helps you combine and compare data stored in different formats, such as Microsoft SQL Server, FoxPro, dBase, and Microsoft Excel. You can use ODBC without actually knowing how data is stored.

How ODBC data sources are used

ODBC uses ODBC data sources to connect to a specific type of database. An *ODBC data source* is a file that contains information about the database location and the database driver. A *database driver* is software that contains information about the type of database and the method used to connect to it.

To access data from a database by using ODBC, Crystal Reports sends the request for data to the ODBC data source, which then passes the request to the database driver. The database driver converts the data request into a form that the database can understand and sends the request to the database. The database then returns the data to the database driver, which then returns it to the data source. The report retrieves the data from the data source and displays it.

Accessing data by using ODBC is often a slow process because the data has to pass through several layers before being displayed.

Do it!

B-1: Discussing ODBC data sources

Questions and answers
1 What technology would you use to combine data from different sources in a report?
Open Database Connectivity (ODBC)
2 What kind of software contains information about the type of database and the method used to connect to it?
A database driver
3 Where is the information about a database's location and driver stored?
In an ODBC data source
4 Name two sources of data to which you can connect by using ODBC data sources.
Answers might include:
• **SQL Server**
• **FoxPro**
• **dBase**
• **Microsoft Excel**

Using ODBC data sources

Explanation   To access data from a database by using ODBC:

1 Create a report by using a Report Wizard.

2 Under Create New Connection, double-click Access/Excel (DAO).

3 Select the database name and type.

4 Add the tables to the Selected Tables list.

5 Follow the Report Wizard steps to create the report.

3/7/2003			
RetailerID	Retailer Name	Region	Total Sales
R-OS-0001	Ordeal Spices	West Coast	$17,000.00
R-OS-0002	Spice World	East Coast	$15,000.00
R-OS-0003	Allspice	Midwest	$22,000.00
R-OS-0004	Chill Corner	Midwest	$21,000.00
R-OS-0005	Spice Wise	East Coast	$12,000.00
R-OS-0006	Winchard Spices	West Coast	$21,000.00
R-OS-0007	The Spice Company	East	$17,000.00
R-OS-0008	Western Spices	West	$16,000.00
R-OS-0009	Spice Up	North	$15,000.00
R-OS-0010	The Spice Corner	South	$22,000.00

Exhibit 4-3: A report containing fields from two data sources

B-2: Creating a report by using an ODBC data source

Here's how	Here's why
1 Open the Crystal Reports Gallery	You'll create a new report by using a Microsoft Access database and an ODBC data source from Microsoft Excel.
Click **OK**	To display the Standard Report Creation Wizard dialog box.
2 Under Create New Connection, double-click **Access/Excel (DAO)**	To display the Access/Excel (DAO) dialog box.
Add the database Outlander Spices	From the current unit folder.
Click **Finish**	To close the Access/Excel (DAO) dialog box and return to the Standard Report Creation Wizard dialog box.
From the Outlander Spices database, add the Retailer table to the Selected Tables list	
3 Under Access/Excel (DAO), double-click **Make New Connection**	To display the Access/Excel (DAO) dialog box.
Click [...]	To display the Open dialog box.
Select **Retailer Sales**	From the current unit folder. You'll display the contents of this Excel file in the report.
Click **Open**	
From the Database Type list, select **Excel 8.0**	
Click **Finish**	
4 Under Retailer Sales.xls, select **Retailer_Sales**, as shown	
Add Retailer_Sales to the Selected Tables list	

Tell students that they will create a sales report for different retailers. The retailer database is in Microsoft Access, but the sales report from the retailers is in a Microsoft Excel worksheet.

5 Click **Next**

To activate the Link screen.

Observe the Link screen

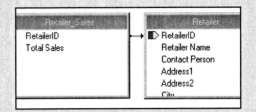

The tables are linked based on the field RetailerID.

6 Click **Next**

The Fields screen is activated.

Under Retailer, add RetailerID, Retailer Name, and Region fields to the Fields to Display list

Expand **Retailer_Sales**

(If necessary.) The fields RetailerID and Total Sales appear under the table name.

Add the Total Sales field to the Fields to Display list

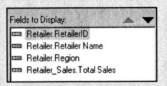

The list should look like this.

Click **Finish**

Click **OK**

(If necessary.) To close the Database Warning message box. This message box states that more than one data source or a stored procedure has been used in the report. The message box further warns you to make sure that no SQL Expression is added and no server-side group-by is performed.

Observe the report

The report appears, as shown in Exhibit 4-3. It contains fields from both data sources.

7 Save the report as **My retailer sales**

Close the report

Topic C: Crystal SQL Designer

Explanation

Creating reports that contain large amounts of information can slow down the process of accessing and displaying data. To speed up the data access process, you can use *Structured Query Language (SQL)* to create queries for retrieving the data you want to see. A *query* is a statement that helps you retrieve data from one or more database tables. To create queries in Crystal Reports, use Crystal SQL Designer. This tool provides two methods for creating queries: SQL syntax and the SQL Expert.

SQL syntax

SQL is a highly complex subject in itself. Tell students that this is just a broad overview.

SQL (often pronounced as "sequel") is a query language that's used to organize, manage, and query large relational databases. SQL syntax is based on *statements*, which are used to perform database operations, such as adding tables or retrieving data. The steps of a SQL statement are called *clauses*. Each clause in a SQL statement, except for the final one, ends with a comma (,). There are four types of clauses, as described in the following sections.

SELECT clauses

A *SELECT* clause specifies the fields to be retrieved from a table. The clause consists of the word "SELECT" followed by a list of fields. If you're using multiple tables in the query, each field name must be prefixed by the table name and a period. However, if a query is based on a single table, then the table name and period are optional. The syntax for a SELECT clause is:

```
SELECT <tablename>.<field 1>,<tablename>.<field 2>....▶
    <tablename>.<field n>
```

The field names in the syntax are always enclosed within grave accents (`). The grave accent key is located just below the Esc key on the keyboard.

FROM clauses

A *FROM* clause specifies names of tables from which data will be queried. In this kind of clause, the word "FROM" is followed by a list of all the tables whose fields were listed in the SELECT clause. You must specify the FROM clause after the SELECT clause, or else the query cannot retrieve data. The syntax is as follows:

```
FROM <tablename>
```

If there is a space in the table name, then you must enclose the full name within grave accents (`), and then follow it with a table name in which underscores (_) replace the space. For example, consider the following query:

```
SELECT Retailers_Table.`Retailer Code`,▶
    Retailers_Table.`Retailer Name`, Retailers_Table.`Sales`
FROM `Retailers Table` Retailers_Table
```

This statement will retrieve data from the Retailer Code, Retailer Name, and Sales fields in the table named Retailers Table.

WHERE clauses

A *WHERE* clause specifies the records or rows that will be retrieved from the table. In this clause, the word "WHERE" is followed by a condition, based on which the specific records should be retrieved from the table. You use comparison operators, such as equals (=), less than (<), or greater than (>), to specify a condition. The syntax is as follows:

```
WHERE <condition>
```

For example:

```
SELECT Retailers_Table.`Retailer Code`,▶
     Retailers_Table.`Retailer Name`, Retailers_Table.`Sales`
FROM `Retailers Table` Retailers_Table
WHERE Retailers_Table.`Sales` > 10000
```

This query would return the specified fields for all records in which the value of the Sales field is greater than 10,000.

ORDER BY clauses

An *ORDER BY* clause sorts the records by the values in a specific field after they have been retrieved from the database. In this clause, the words "ORDER BY" are followed by a field name and the sort order, which can be ascending or descending. The syntax is as follows:

```
ORDER BY <field> <order>
```

You can use the keyword "ASC" to specify ascending order, or "DESC" to specify descending order. For example, consider this query:

```
SELECT Retailers_Table.`Retailer Code`,▶
     Retailers_Table.`Retailer Name`, Retailers_Table.`Sales`
FROM `Retailers Table` Retailers_Table
WHERE Retailers_Table.`Sales` > 10000
ORDER BY Retailers_Table.`Retailer Name` ASC
```

This query is the same as in the preceding example, except that the returned data will be sorted in ascending, or alphabetical, order based on the field Retailer Name.

Creating a query by writing SQL syntax

Every SQL statement must contain both SELECT and FROM clauses. The WHERE and ORDER BY clauses are optional.

To create a query by writing SQL syntax:

1 Start Crystal SQL Designer.

2 Click New to open the New Query dialog box.

3 Click the Enter SQL Statement Directly button to open the Log On Server dialog box.

4 Select the type of database to connect to, and click OK.

5 Select the database you want to connect to, and click OK. A message box will inform you that you have successfully logged on to the ODBC data source.

6 Click OK to open the Enter SQL Statement dialog box.

7 Enter the SQL statement, and click OK.

8 A message box asks whether you want to process the query now. Click Yes to view the query results.

Customer Code	Customer	Address	City	State
▶ C002	Mark Peterson	4691 SE Amity Rd	Amity	OR
C003	Rita Greg	74 4th St	Astoria	OR
C004	Anna Morris	2265 Exchange St	Astoria	OR
C005	Monica Dukes	7791 Albus Rd SE	Aumsville	OR
C006	Nikki Cleary	8225 Ce Clatsop St	Portland	OR
C007	Annie Philips	672 Sasy Ln S	Aumsville	OR
C008	Paul Anderson	1408 N Terry St	Portland	OR
C009	Jesse Bennet	815 SE Topaz Ave	Portland	OR
C001	Jamie Morrison	2885 Walnut St NE	Aurora	OR

Exhibit 4-4: All the customer records, which were retrieved by using the query

Customer Code	Customer Name	Address	City	State
▶ C004	Anna Morris	2265 Exchange St	Astoria	OR
C003	Rita Greg	74 4th St	Astoria	OR

Exhibit 4-5: The customer records sorted in ascending order

Do it!

C-1:   Using SQL syntax to retrieve report data

Here's how	Here's why
1 Choose **Start, Programs, Crystal Data Compatibility Tools, Crystal SQL Designer**	You'll create a simple SQL query to retrieve customer data from the Outlander Spices database.
2 Click 	To open the New Query dialog box.
3 Click 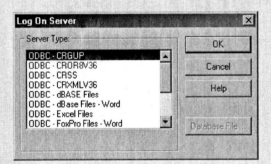	To open the Log On Server dialog box.
4 From the list, select **ODBC - MS Access Database** Click **OK**	To open the Select Database dialog box.
5 Select **Outlander Spices.mdb** Click **OK**	From the current unit folder.
	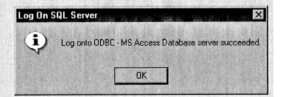
	A message box informs you that you have successfully logged on to the database.
Click **OK**	To open the Enter SQL Statement dialog box.

Tell students that Outlander Spices also sells directly to customers. The Vice President of Sales wants to see customer-related data in a report.

This is the Enter SQL statement directly button.

Tell students that they can also copy this code from SQL.txt.

TIPS ✔ *Point out that line breaks are ignored in SQL syntax. It can be easier to read a query when each table or field name is on its own line.*

Point out that the grave accent key is located just below the Esc key on the keyboard.

6   In the SQL box, enter the SQL statement shown

```
SQL:
SELECT
Direct_Customers.`Customer Code`,
Direct_Customers.`Customer Name`,
Direct_Customers.`Address`,
Direct_Customers.`City`,
Direct_Customers.`State`

FROM
`Direct Customers` Direct_Customers
```

Observe the SELECT clause

The SELECT clause specifies that the Customer Code, Customer Name, Address, City, and State fields from the Direct_Customers table should be retrieved. Notice that the field names are enclosed within grave accents (`).

Observe the FROM clause

It specifies the database table from which the fields will be retrieved ("Direct Customers"). The clause also specifies the name that will be used for the table within the query itself ("Direct_Customers"), in which an underscore replaces the space.

Click **OK**

A message box asks whether you want to process the query now.

Click **Yes**

The records for all customers appear in the window, as shown in Exhibit 4-4.

7   Choose **Edit**, **Query...**

To open the Enter SQL Statement dialog box. You'll alter the query to select only those records for which the City field value is "Astoria."

Deselect the query text

⚠ *Make sure that students enclose the city name within single quotes, not grave accents.*

8   Enter the WHERE clause, as shown

```
FROM
`Direct Customers`Direct_Customers

WHERE
Direct_Customers.`City`='Astoria'
```

(After the FROM clause. Be sure to enclose the city name in single quotes.) This WHERE clause specifies that the query should retrieve only those records in which the city is "Astoria."

Click **OK**

A message box asks whether you want to process the query now.

Click **Yes**

To process the query. The records for customers from Astoria are displayed. There are two. Rita Greg's record appears first.

9 Edit the query	(Choose Edit, Query.) Next, you'll add an ORDER BY clause to sort the records on the Customer Name field.
| Enter the ORDER BY clause, as shown | ```
WHERE
Direct_Customers.`City`='Astoria'

ORDER BY
Direct_Customers.`Customer Name` ASC
``` |
	To sort the records on the Customer Name field. You use "ASC" to specify that the records should be sorted in ascending order.
Click **OK**, then click **Yes**	To process the query now. The customer records are sorted in ascending, or alphabetical, order by first name. The record of Anna Morris appears first, as shown in Exhibit 4-5.
10 Click 🖫	To open the File Save As dialog box.
Select the current unit folder	
Edit the File name box to read **My custquery**	To save the query with a .qry extension.
Click **OK**	
Choose **File**, **Close**	To close the query.
```

The SQL Expert

If you're not comfortable using SQL, you can use the Crystal SQL Expert to create SQL queries. The SQL Expert walks you through a series of steps to create a query, and then automatically generates the necessary SQL clauses. To create a query by using this method, open the New Query dialog box in the Crystal SQL Designer, and then click the Use SQL Expert button. The SQL Expert has six tabs that guide you through the steps to create a query. These tabs are described in the following sections.

Tables tab

On the Tables tab, you select the database and tables to be used in the query. This step is similar to using the FROM clause in SQL. You can create the query by using either a dictionary or an ODBC database. To create a query by using a Dictionary, click the Dictionary button, select a dictionary file name, and click OK. To create a query by using an ODBC database, click the SQL/ODBC button, follow the steps to connect to the data source, and then select the tables.

Links tab

The Links tab appears only if you have selected multiple tables. It helps you link the tables on a common field. The Smart Linking button will attempt to automatically link tables based on similar fields.

Fields tab

On the Fields tab, you select the fields for the query to retrieve. This step is similar to using the SELECT clause in SQL. To use a field in a query, select it from the Database Fields list and click Add. You can also click the All button to add all the fields.

Sort tab

The Sort tab is used to specify the field on which to sort records. It's similar to using the ORDER BY clause in SQL. To specify a sort field, select it from the Database Fields list and click Add. The Order list will then appear; from this list, you can select ascending or descending order. You can sort on multiple fields.

Select tab

On the Select tab, you can specify conditions for record selection (as you would in the WHERE clause of a SQL statement). To do so, select a field from the Database Fields list, and click Add to add it to the Select Fields list. Two new lists appear. In the first, you can select either "is" or "is not." In the second list, you can specify a comparison operator, such as "greater than" or "less than." When you select an item from this list, a third list appears, which contains data from the selected field. Select a value to complete the condition.

SQL tab

The SQL tab displays the SQL statement generated by the SQL Expert. If necessary, you can modify the statement here.

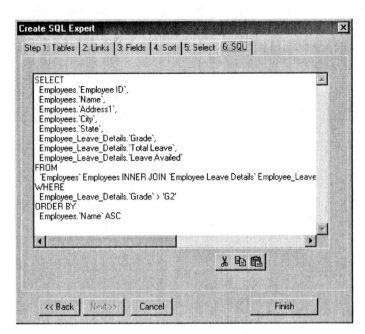

Exhibit 4-6: A query created in the SQL Expert

Employee ID	Name	Address1	City	State	Grade	Total Leave	Leave Availed
E039	Diana Stone	15 SE 73rd Ave.	Portland	OR	G3	30	20
E041	Kevin Meyers	23 SW 59th Ave.	Portland	OR	G4	25	20
E024	Kristin White	450 Upper Nestucca Riv Rd.	Beaver	OR	G3	30	5
E034	Rob Dukes	45 Staten Island	Manhattan	NY	G4	25	23

Exhibit 4-7: The records of employees with grades higher than G2

Do it!

C-2: Using the SQL Expert to create a SQL statement

Here's how	Here's why
1 Open the New Query dialog box	Click New.
Click	(The Use SQL Expert button.) To open the Create SQL Expert dialog box with the Step 1: Tables tab activated.
Click	To open the Choose SQL Table dialog box.
2 Under SQL Tables, from the list, select **Employees**	
Click **Add**	To add the table to the query.
Add the table **Employee Leave Details**	
Click **Done**	To close the dialog box and return to the Create SQL Expert. The 2: Links tab is activated.
3 Click **Smart Linking**	To link the tables on the common field.
Click **Next**	To activate the 3: Fields tab.
4 From the Employees table, add the Employee ID, Name, Address1, City, and State fields	Select the fields and click Add.
From the Employee_Leave_Details table, add the Grade, Total Leave, and Leave Availed fields	
Click **Next**	To activate the 4: Sort tab.
5 Add the **Employees.Name** field	(Scroll down the list to locate the field.) To sort records based on this field. The order list appears, and ascending order is selected.
Click **Next**	To activate the 5: Select tab.

	6 Add the **Grade** field	(Scroll down the list to view the field.) Two new lists appear below the Database Fields list.
	From the second list, select **greater than**	
	From the third list, select **G2**	A third list appears.
		To select the records for only those employees who have a grade higher than G2.
	7 Click **Next**	To activate the 6: SQL tab.
Tell students to deselect the query text.	Observe the SQL statement	The SQL Expert created all the clauses, as shown in Exhibit 4-6, based upon your choices on the tabs.
	8 Click **Finish**	A message box appears asking whether you want to process the query now.
Tell student they might need to scroll to the right to see all the field columns.	Click **Yes**	The data for employees with grades higher than G2 appears in the Crystal SQL Designer, as shown in Exhibit 4-7.
	9 Save the query as **My empquery**	In the current unit folder.
	Close the query	Choose File, Close.
	Close Crystal SQL Designer	Choose File, Exit.

In the second list area:

is ▾ | greater than ▾
☐ or equal to

Using queries

Explanation

After you create a query, you can use it to create a report. To do so:

1 Open the Crystal Reports Gallery.
2 Click OK to open the Report Wizard.
3 In the Report Wizard, double-click Crystal Queries to display the Open dialog box.
4 Select a query file, and click Open. Add the query to the Selected Tables list.
5 Follow the Report Wizard steps to create the report.

Point out that students would have to adjust column widths to make the report look exactly like this exhibit.

3/8/2003							
Employee ID	Name	Address1	City	State	Grade	Total Leave	Leave Availed
E039	Diana Stone	15 SE 73rd Ave.	Portland	OR	G3	30	20
E041	Kevin Meyers	23 SW 59th Ave.	Portland	OR	G4	25	20
E024	Kristin White	450 Upper Nestucca Riv Rd.	Beaver	OR	G3	30	5
E034	Rob Dukes	45 Staten Island	Manhattan	NY	G4	25	23

Exhibit 4-8: The report created by using the My empquery query

Do it!

C-3: Creating a report based on a query

Here's how	Here's why
1 Activate the Crystal Reports window	If necessary.
Open Crystal Reports Gallery	
Click **OK**	
2 Expand **Create New Connection**	If necessary.
Double-click **Crystal Queries**	To display the Open dialog box.
Select **My empquery**	From the current unit folder.
Click **Open**	
3 Under My empquery, double-click **Query**	To add Query to the Selected Tables list.
Click **Next**	The Fields tab is activated.
4 Add all the fields to the Fields to Display list	The fields appear with a Query prefix.
5 Click **Finish**	
Arrange the report fields	To create a report, as shown in Exhibit 4-8.
6 Save the report as **My employee report**	In the current unit folder.
7 Close the report	

Topic D: Report alerts

Explanation

In some cases, you might want report information only when certain conditions are met. To do so, you first need to evaluate the conditions. You can do this by using the *report alerts* feature. By using this feature, you can create report-specific formulas that evaluate conditions you specify and display messages only if those conditions are true.

Creating report alerts

You create report alerts by using the Create Alert dialog box. To open it, choose Reports, Alerts, Create or Modify Alerts, and then click New. In this dialog box, you specify a name for the alert, the condition that will trigger it, and the message it will display.

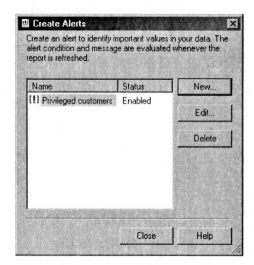

Exhibit 4-9: The Create Alerts dialog box

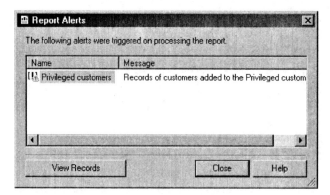

Exhibit 4-10: The Report Alerts dialog box

```
Customer Order Report

Order Details ID  OrderID    Product ID  Customer ID  Quantity (In Packs)  Unit Price (Per Pack)  Sales Value
         9         O-OS-012    P010        C008                55                 $23.00             $1,265.00
        25         O-OS-012    P019        C005                35                 $30.00             $1,050.00
        30         O-OS-015    P015        C008                45                 $25.00             $1,125.00
```

Exhibit 4-11: The records of customers whose sales value is greater than $1000

Do it!

D-1: Creating a report alert

Here's how	Here's why
1 Open Customer order report	(From the current unit folder.) The sales manager wants to create a privileged-customers list that will include the records of customers who have spent more than $1000.
Activate the Design tab	
2 Choose **Report, Alerts, Create or Modify Alerts...**	To open the Create Alerts dialog box.
Click **New**	To open the Create Alert dialog box.
3 In the Name box, enter **Privileged customers**	
In the Message box, enter **Records of customers added to the Privileged customers list**	To specify the default message that will appear whenever the alert is triggered.
Verify that Enabled is checked	
4 Click **Condition**	To open the Formula Workshop – Alert Condition Formula Editor window, where you'll enter an alert condition formula.
In the Formula text window, type **{Customer-Order.Sales Value}>1000**	This formula will test for customers whose sales value is greater than 1000.
5 Check the formula, save it, and then close the Alert Condition Formula Editor	
6 Click **OK**	The Create Alerts dialog box should look like Exhibit 4-9.
Click **Close**	

7 Preview the report

8 Choose **Report, Refresh Report Data**

Click **OK** — To close the message box. The Report Alerts dialog box appears, as shown in Exhibit 4-10. It lists the name and message of the alert that was triggered upon processing the report.

9 Click **View Records** — To view the records of customers who satisfy the condition specified in the alert. A new tab, Privileged customers, is added next to the Preview tab. Notice that the Sales Value field in all the listed records is greater than $1000, as shown in Exhibit 4-11.

10 Activate the Design tab

Save the report as **My customer order report**

Modifying report alerts

Explanation

To modify a report alert, you open the Create Alerts dialog box, select the alert you want to edit, and click Edit. In the Edit Alert dialog box, you can change the name, message, or condition for the alert.

Customer Order Report

Order Details ID	OrderID	Product ID	Customer ID	Quantity (In Packs)	Unit Price (Per Pack)	Sales Value
4	O-OS-013	P015	C006	40	$25.00	$1,000.00
9	O-OS-012	P010	C008	55	$23.00	$1,265.00
25	O-OS-012	P019	C005	35	$30.00	$1,050.00
30	O-OS-015	P015	C008	45	$25.00	$1,125.00

Exhibit 4-12: The records in which the sales value is greater than or equal to $1000

D-2:   Modifying a report alert

Here's how	Here's why
1 Open the Create Alerts dialog box	(Choose Report, Alerts, Create or Modify Alerts.) An alert box warns you that you cannot perform the command and keep the Alerting tabs, and that if you continue, the Alerting tabs will be closed.
Click **OK**	To close the alert box. You'll modify the report alert.
2 Click **Edit**	To open the Edit Alert dialog box.
3 Click **Condition**	To open the Formula Workshop – Alert Condition Formula Editor dialog box.
In the Formula text window, edit the formula to read:	

```
{Customer-Order.Sales Value}>= 1000
```

Check the formula, save it, and then close the window	
4 Click **OK**	(In the Edit Alert dialog box.) To accept the modifications and close the dialog box.
Click **Close**	To close the Create Alerts dialog box.
5 Preview the report	
Refresh the report	(Choose Report, Refresh Report Data.) The refresh data message appears.
Click **OK**	To close the message box and display the Report Alerts dialog box.
View the selected records	(Click View Records.) The record for Order Details ID 4 has been added to the list because its sales value is equal to $1000, as shown in Exhibit 4-12.
6 Activate the Design tab	
Update the report	

Deleting report alerts

Explanation

You can delete any or all of the report alerts in a report. To delete an alert, in the Create Alerts dialog box, select the alert and click Delete.

Do it!

D-3: Deleting a report alert

Here's how	Here's why
1 Open the Create Alerts dialog box	A message box appears, prompting you to close the Alerting tabs.
Click **OK**	To close the Alerting tabs.
2 Verify that the Privileged customers alert is selected	You'll delete this alert.
Click **Delete**	
Click **Close**	
3 Preview the report	
4 Choose **Report**, **Alerts**, **Triggered Alerts...**	To open the Report Alerts dialog box. Notice that the box is empty.
Click **Close**	
5 Update and close the report	

Tell students that if they refresh the report now, the Report Alert dialog box will not appear.

Unit summary: Advanced data access techniques

Topic A In this unit, you learned how to use the **Crystal Dictionary Expert** to create a **dictionary** that provides only the data relevant to specific users. Then, you learned how to create and modify a report based on a dictionary.

Topic B Next, you learned how to use **ODBC data sources** to access data from different types of databases simultaneously. You also learned how to use ODBC data sources to create a report.

Topic C Then, you learned how to use **SQL syntax** to create **SQL queries**. You also learned how to use **Crystal SQL Designer** to create SQL queries without having to write SQL statements yourself.

Topic D Finally, you learned how to **create**, **modify**, and **delete report alerts**. You learned that report alerts can display messages when certain conditions are met.

Independent practice activity

1 Create a dictionary from the Retailer table of the Outlander Spices database. Add the Retailer ID, Retailer name, Contact Person, and Region fields to the dictionary. Change the name of the table in the dictionary to **Retailers for different regions**, as shown in Exhibit 4-13. Collect sample data for all the fields in the dictionary.

2 Save the dictionary as **My retailers dictionary**.

3 Close the Crystal Dictionaries window.

4 Create a report by using the My retailers dictionary. Add all the fields available in the dictionary to the report.

5 Preview the report and compare it to Exhibit 4-14.

6 Save the report as **My retailers report**, and then close it.

7 Use the SQL Expert in Crystal SQL Designer to create a new query based on the tables Inventory items and Inventory stock from the Outlander Spices database. (This is a Microsoft Access database.) Link the tables. The query should retrieve the Item No, Item Name, and Category fields from the Inventory items table, and retrieve the Quantity purchased (In Packs), Quantity Used (In Packs), and Reorder Level Quantity fields from the Inventory stock table. The query records should be sorted on the Quantity Used (In Packs) field in descending order. Specify a condition to select only those records in which Quantity Purchased (In Packs) is greater than 10,000. When you are done, compare your results to Exhibit 4-15.

8 Save the query as **My inventory stock query** (in the current unit folder).

9 Close Crystal SQL Designer.

10 Create a report based on the My inventory stock query. Add the Item Name, Category, Quantity Purchased (In Packs), and Reorder Level Quantity fields. Your report should look like Exhibit 4-16.

11 Save the report as **My inventory report**.

12 In the My inventory report, create a report alert called **Reorder level** that will be triggered if the Reorder Level Quantity is below 1300. The default message should read **The Reorder Level Quantity is below 1300**. View those records. The report should appear as shown in Exhibit 4-17.

13 Update and close the report.

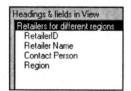

Exhibit 4-13: The table name changed in the dictionary

RetailerID	Retailer Name	Contact Person	Region
R-OS-0006	Winchard Spices	Dave Thomas	West Coast
R-OS-0007	The Spice Company	Warren Hyde	East
R-OS-0008	Western Spices	Cavin Andrews	West
R-OS-0009	Spice Up	Rita Greg	North
R-OS-0010	The Spice Corner	Rachel Jones	South
R-OS-0001	Ordeal Spices	Shane Thomas	West Coast
R-OS-0002	Spice World	Jane Andrews	East Coast
R-OS-0003	Allspice	Julia Joseph	Midwest
R-OS-0004	Chill Corner	David Thomas	Midwest
R-OS-0005	Spice Wise	Roger Williams	East Coast

Exhibit 4-14: The report created after step 5 of the Independent Practice Activity

I014	Chip davis DRY brushless baste	Rubs and Marinades	17,000	16,000	1,100
I011	Arizona gunslinger	Hot Sauces	14,500	14,000	1,200
I020	Almond flavoring oil	Flavoring Oils	15,000	14,000	1,500
I021	Asbirin hot sauce	Hot Sauces	16,000	14,000	1,100
I002	Anise flavoring oil	Flavoring Oils	15,000	12,000	1,500
I005	Blueberry flavoring oil	Flavoring Oils	14,000	12,000	1,250
I013	Acid rain	Hot Sauces	14,250	12,000	1,500
I019	Amaretto flavoring oil	Flavoring Oils	14,000	12,000	1,200
I012	Garlic flavour wing sauce	Hot Sauces	14,350	12,000	1,400
I009	Amazon pepper fiery red hot sauce	Hot Sauces	12,000	11,000	1,000
I018	Honey mustard	Rubs and Marinades	12,000	11,000	1,100
I015	New Orleans cajun	Rubs and Marinades	12,000	10,000	1,200
I001	Banana flavoring oil	Flavoring Oils	12,000	10,000	1,000
I004	Apricot flavoring oil	Flavoring Oils	12,000	10,000	1,200
I010	Pepper ranch hot wing sauce	Hot Sauces	11,000	9,800	1,150
I017	Chef's basic	Rubs and Marinades	11,000	8,000	1,500

Exhibit 4-15: The query created in step 7 of the Independent Practice Activity

Item Name	Category	Quantity Purchased (In Packs)	Reorder Level Quantity
Chip davis DRY brushless ba	Rubs and Marinades	17,000	1,100
Arizona gunslinger	Hot Sauces	14,500	1,200
Almond flavoring oil	Flavoring Oils	15,000	1,500
Asbirin hot sauce	Hot Sauces	16,000	1,100
Anise flavoring oil	Flavoring Oils	15,000	1,500
Blueberry flavoring oil	Flavoring Oils	14,000	1,250
Acid rain	Hot Sauces	14,250	1,500
Amaretto flavoring oil	Flavoring Oils	14,000	1,200
Garlic flavour wing sauce	Hot Sauces	14,350	1,400
Amazon pepper fiery red hot	Hot Sauces	12,000	1,000
Honey mustard	Rubs and Marinades	12,000	1,100
New Orleans cajun	Rubs and Marinades	12,000	1,200
Banana flavoring oil	Flavoring Oils	12,000	1,000
Apricot flavoring oil	Flavoring Oils	12,000	1,200
Pepper ranch hot wing sauce	Hot Sauces	11,000	1,150
Chef's basic	Rubs and Marinades	11,000	1,500

Exhibit 4-16: The report created after step 10 of the Independent Practice Activity

Item Name	Category	Quantity Purchased (In Packs)	Reorder Level Quantity
Chip davis DRY brushless ba	Rubs and Marinades	17,000	1,100
Arizona gunslinger	Hot Sauces	14,500	1,200
Asbirin hot sauce	Hot Sauces	16,000	1,100
Blueberry flavoring oil	Flavoring Oils	14,000	1,250
Amaretto flavoring oil	Flavoring Oils	14,000	1,200
Amazon pepper fiery red hot	Hot Sauces	12,000	1,000
Honey mustard	Rubs and Marinades	12,000	1,100
New Orleans cajun	Rubs and Marinades	12,000	1,200
Banana flavoring oil	Flavoring Oils	12,000	1,000
Apricot flavoring oil	Flavoring Oils	12,000	1,200
Pepper ranch hot wing sauce	Hot Sauces	11,000	1,150

Exhibit 4-17: The report after step 12 of the Independent Practice Activity

Unit 5

Charts and maps

Unit time: 70 minutes

Complete this unit, and you'll know how to:

A Create and modify charts to provide a visual representation of data.

B Create and customize maps to represent data geographically.

Topic A: Working with charts

Explanation

You add charts to a report to provide a visual representation of data. Charts can help users interpret and analyze data more effectively than they can by viewing a set of records. Charts are linked to report data. As a result, any changes you make in a report's data will be reflected in the chart.

Creating charts

You can create several types of charts, depending on the type of data you want to display. The following table describes some of the available chart types:

Type	Description
Bar	Displays bars of different heights to represent values for sets of data. You use bar charts to display and compare single or multiple sets of data.
Line	Plots data as a series of dots joined by a line. This type of chart is useful for analyzing trends. For example, you might use a line chart to view profit trends for the last 10 years.
Area	Plots data as color-filled areas on the chart. This type of chart is useful for showing one type of data as a sum of other types. For example, you might want to show the total costs for a year as the sum of production costs and fixed costs.
Pie	Plots a single set of data, which is represented by divisions of a circle (or slices of a pie). For example, you could use a pie chart to represent four regions' sales totals as percentages of the total sales.
Gantt	Plots only the date values. The data is represented in a horizontal bar chart. For example, you might want to show the schedule of your project.
Gauge	Plots data graphically on a gauge. The data is shown as a set of points and is useful for showing only one group of data. For example, you might want to use a Gantt chart to show the percentages of total inventory.

The Chart Expert

The Chart Expert has several tabs that guide you through the process of creating charts. You use the Chart Expert to specify the type of chart, the data to be plotted, and the chart title, among several other things. Here's what you do:

1   Choose Insert, Chart to open the Chart Expert.
2   In the Type tab, select the needed chart type.
3   Activate the Data tab, and specify the data to be plotted on the chart.
4   Activate the Text tab, and specify a chart title.
5   Click OK to insert the chart.

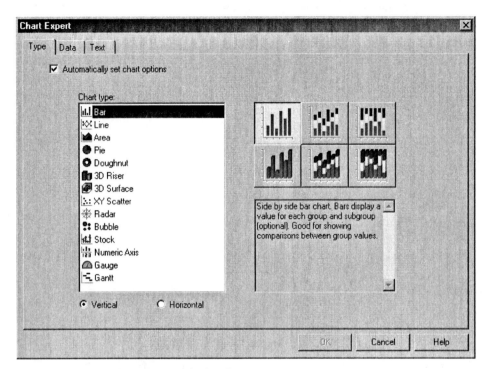

Exhibit 5-1: The Chart Expert dialog box

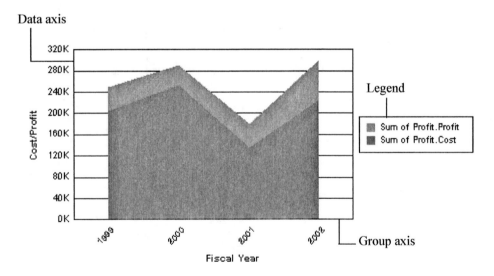

Exhibit 5-2: The Cost profit analysis chart

A-1: Creating a chart

Here's how	Here's why
1 Open Cost profit analysis	(From the current unit folder.) The Vice President of Finance wants to present a chart showing cost/profit data for 1999–2002.
Activate the Design tab	
2 Choose **Insert**, **Chart...**	To open the Chart Expert dialog box. The Type tab gives you several choices for the type of chart, as shown in Exhibit 5-1.
Clear **Automatically set chart options**	Notice that two tabs, Axes and Options, appear.
From the Chart type list, select **Area**	You'll create an Area chart.
3 Click the **Data** tab	Here, you specify the field values to be plotted on the chart.
Under Placement, select **Footer**	To place the chart in the Report Footer section.
4 From the Available fields list, select **Profit.Year**	
Click as shown	

Point out that the Chart Expert offers several formats for each chart type.

To add the Year field to the On change of list. This means that the years will appear on the horizontal or Group axis of the chart.

From the Available fields list, select **Profit.Cost**

Click as shown

To add the Cost field to the Show value(s) list. This means that the chart will show the sums of values from the Cost field for each year as one series on the chart plotted against the vertical or Data axis.

5 Add Profit.Profit to the Show value(s) list, as shown

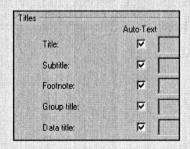

To plot the sums of the Profit values as another series, along with the sums of the Cost values.

6 Activate the Text tab

On this tab you can specify titles for the entire chart, the axes, and other chart elements. The Auto-Text option tells the Chart Expert to automatically assign titles for the elements.

Under Titles, clear **Group title**

To make the Group title box available.

In the box, enter **Fiscal Year**

This will be the title for the horizontal axis.

7 Under Titles, clear **Data title**

To make the Data title box available.

In the box, enter **Cost/Profit**

This will be the title for the vertical axis.

Click **OK**

To insert the chart.

8 Deselect the chart

Preview the report

The chart appears as shown in Exhibit 5-2. It displays data for the years 1999 to 2002, with years plotted on the Group axis, and cost/profit plotted on the Data axis. The chart displays cost data in the blue area and profit data in the red area.

9 Save the report as **My cost profit analysis**

Modifying charts

Explanation

After you create a chart, you can modify it by using the Chart Expert, the Chart menu, or both. To modify a chart by using the Chart Expert, select the chart and choose Format, Chart Expert. You can then add data points, set the range and scale of the chart's axes, or make any other needed changes.

Data points are small labels that show the actual values plotted on the graph. The *range* sets a minimum and maximum limit for the data to be plotted on a chart. For example, you can set the minimum range to 2000 and the maximum range to 4000 if the data values to be plotted on the chart range from 2000 to 4000. Using a range will accentuate any trends shown in the chart. By default, the minimum range limit is zero. The chart's *scale* specifies the division of values on the data axes.

The Chart menu

You use the Chart menu to format each component of a chart individually. You can also use the Chart menu to modify chart colors and to save the chart as a template. A *template* stores all the formatting—such as color, scale, and range—that has been applied to the chart. You can then use the template to create another chart with the same formatting.

The following table describes some of the commands in the Chart menu:

Command	What it does
Formatting	Opens the Formatting dialog box, which shows different formatting options depending on the component selected. This button is active only when a chart component is selected.
Titles	Opens the Titles dialog box, which you can use to change the chart and axis titles.
Template	Opens the Choose a Chart Type dialog box, which you can use to select a template to apply to the chart.

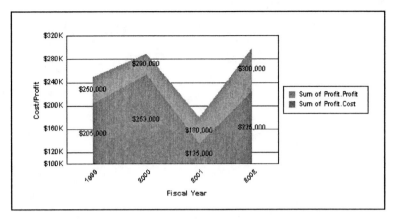

Exhibit 5-3: The Cost profit analysis chart with data points

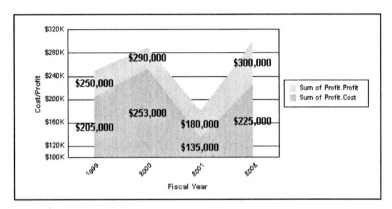

Exhibit 5-4: The Cost profit analysis with modified colors and data points

Do it!

A-2: Modifying a chart

Here's how	Here's why
1 Activate the Design tab	
Select the chart	(If necessary.) You'll use the Chart Expert and Analyzer to modify the chart.
2 Choose **Format**, **Chart Expert...**	To open the Chart Expert dialog box.
3 Activate the Axes tab	
Under Data values, check **Auto scale**	To specify that the Chart Expert should automatically select the scale for the values plotted on the Data axis.
Under Data values, clear **Auto range**	You'll modify the data range on the Data axis. The Min, Max, and Number format boxes are now available.
In the Min box, enter **100000**	By raising the minimum of the chart's range, you can accentuate the differences between the plotted values.
In the Max box, enter **320000**	To keep the maximum of the range the same.
From the Number format list, select **$1K**, as shown	
	To format the data values so that they appear with a $ sign and a "K" on the Data axis.
4 Activate the Options tab	
Under Data points, select **Show value**	To display the values of the data plotted in the chart.
From the Number format list, select **$1**, as shown	
Click **OK**	

5 Preview the report

All the values now appear as labels by plotted points, along with dollar signs, as shown in Exhibit 5-3. These labels are called *data points*.

Observe the Data axis

The scale range now begins at $100K, which has the effect of exaggerating the differences between the values in the chart.

6 Select the chart

If necessary.

Point to a data value, as shown

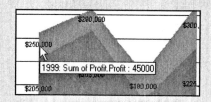

The value appears in a screen tip.

7 Click the Cost area of the chart

(The blue area.) To select the plotted Cost data.

8 Choose **Chart**, **Chart Options**, **Selected Item...**

To open the Formatting dialog box. You'll change the color of the selected area.

Select the R7C7 color, as shown

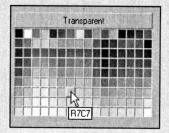

Click **OK**

To change the color of the Cost area to the selected color.

Change the color of the Profit area to Yellow

(Select the Profit area and choose Chart, Chart Options, Selected Item.) In the Formatting dialog box, select R1C8 from the Color palette.

9 Select the indicated data point

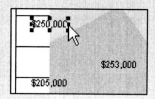

10	Open the Formatting dialog box	You'll change the font of the data point.
	From the Size list, select **10**	To change the size of the data points.
	From the Style list, select **Bold**	To make the data points appear bold.
	Click **OK**	The cost and sale values now appear larger and bold.
11	Observe the report	The chart should look like Exhibit 5-4.
12	Update and close the report	

Tell students to deselect the chart.

Topic B: Working with maps

Explanation

You use maps to represent data geographically. For example, you could use a map to show how customers are distributed across a specific city or state. To add a map to a report, use the Map Expert. Because a map is always linked to a report, the data represented on the map will change when you change the associated report data.

Creating maps

You can create several types of maps:

- **Ranged map**—Displays areas in different colors based on the range of values within which the data associated with the areas falls. For example, you could have a ranged map in which regions with more customers will appear in a darker color as compared to regions with fewer customers.

- **Dot Density map**—Displays dots for each item in a region. In a Dot Density map, a larger number of dots in a specific region represents a higher value. Such maps are useful for population census data.

- **Graduated map**—Is similar to a Ranged map, except that instead of displaying regions in different colors, a Graduated map displays symbols of different sizes within the regions.

The Map Expert

To create a map, use the Map Expert. It has three tabs that guide you through the process. Here's what you do:

1   Choose Insert, Map to open the Map Expert. The Data tab will be activated.

2   Under Placement, specify whether the map should be placed in the header or the footer.

3   From the Available fields list, specify the fields to be added to the Geographic field box. The geographic field specifies the geographic areas for which the values should appear on the map. For example, this field could contain a list of cities.

4   From the Available fields list, specify the fields to be added to the Map values box. The Map values specify the corresponding values based on which the geographic fields will appear on the map. For example, the field to be added to this list could be the number of customers in a city.

5   Activate the Type tab. Here you specify the map type: Ranged, Dot Density, or Graduated.

6   Activate the Text tab. Here you can specify a title and legend for the map.

7   Click OK to add the map to the report.

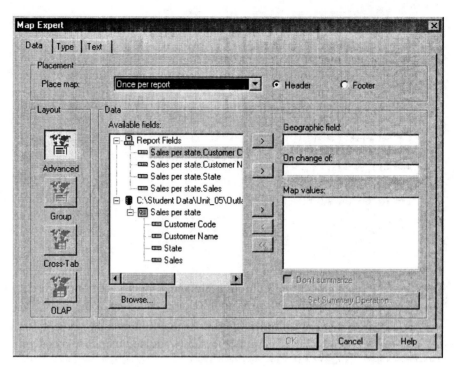

Exhibit 5-5: The Map Expert dialog box

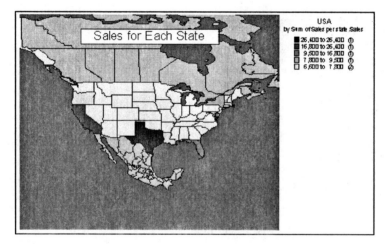

Exhibit 5-6: A map displaying sales by state

Do it!   **B-1:   Using the Map Expert to create a map**

Here's how	Here's why
1 Open Sales for each state	You'll add a map to this report to display sales distribution across the United States.
Activate the Design tab	
2 Choose **Insert**, **Map...**	To open the Map Expert, as shown in Exhibit 5-5. By default, the Data tab is activated.
Under Placement, select **Footer**	You'll place the map in the Report Footer section.
3 Under Report Fields, select **Sales per state.State**	
Click as shown	Geographic field:
	To add this field to the Geographic field box. This is the field from which geographical regions will be selected for the map.
4 Under Report Fields, select **Sales per state.Sales**	
Click as shown	Map values:
	To add this field to the Map values list. The states will be filled with different colors based on the values in this field.
Observe the Map values list	Map values: Sum of Sales per state.Sales
	The colors of the states will be determined by the total sales for each state.

5 Activate the Type tab

By default, Ranged is selected. This type of map will display the states in different colors based on the range of values in the Sales field. The states where total sales are higher will appear in darker colors.

From the Color of highest interval palette, select Maroon, as shown

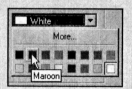

The states within the highest sales range will be filled with this color.

From the Color of lowest interval palette, select Yellow, as shown

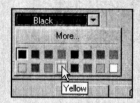

The states within the lowest sales range will be filled with this color. States whose sales amount falls between the highest and lowest ranges will appear in shades between the selected Maroon and Yellow colors.

6 Activate the Text tab

In the Map title box, enter **Sales for Each State**

Click **OK**

To add the map to the Report Footer section.

7 Deselect the map and preview the report

(Scroll down to view the map.) The map should look like Exhibit 5-6. Notice that Texas, California, and Florida have the most sales. There are some sales in New York and the least amount in Oregon and Louisiana. There are no sales in the other 44 states.

8 Save the report as **My sales for each state**

Customizing maps

Explanation

After you create a map, you can modify it by using the Map Expert or the Map menu.

The Map menu

Here are some of the ways in which you can modify a map:

- The Resolve Mismatch option is available only when the map does not recognize some of the values in a geographic field. Use this option to match the map areas with the geographical field's values. To do this, choose Map, Resolve Mismatch to open the Resolve Map Mismatch dialog box, where you can match map keywords with field values.

- You can use Zoom In or Zoom Out to see enlarged or smaller views of the map area.

- You can use the Pan option to move the map with the Panning cursor. This feature is useful when you have a large map and you want to bring a specific area into view.

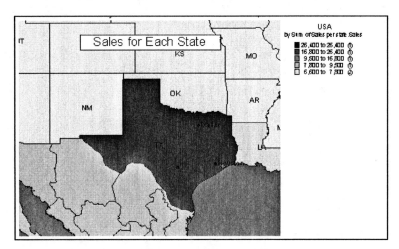

Exhibit 5-7: The enlarged map with state abbreviations

B-2: Customizing a map

Here's how	Here's why
1 Select the map	There are only a few states for which the data appears on the map. You'll use the Map menu to customize the map so that only those states appear in the preview.
2 Choose **Map, Zoom In**	The Zoom In command is used to enlarge the map.
Click Colorado, as shown	
	To enlarge the map with Colorado at the center.
Deselect the map	
3 Observe the report	An enlarged view of only a selected area of the map appears.
4 Select the map	
Click the Zoom In command	Choose Map, Zoom In.
5 Click Texas, as shown	
	To further enlarge the map area.

Tell students that the Vice President of Sales wants to view and compare sales for only certain states.

6 Right-click the map

To display the shortcut menu. You'll add state name abbreviations to the map.

Choose **Layers...**

To open the Layer Control dialog box.

From the Layers list, select **USA**

Under Properties, check **Automatic Labels**

Click **OK**

Abbreviations of state names now appear on the map.

Tell students to deselect the map.

7 Observe the report

It should now look like Exhibit 5-7.

8 Update and close the report

Unit summary: Charts and maps

Topic A
In this unit, you learned how to create **charts** by using the **Chart Expert**. Then, you learned how to modify charts by using the Chart Expert and the **Chart menu**.

Topic B
Finally, you learned that **maps** permit you to show data geographically. You learned how to create maps by using the **Map Expert**, and how to customize them by using the **Map** menu.

Independent practice activity

1 Open **Quarterly sales report**.

2 Insert a Bar chart for Quarterly sales in the Report Footer section. Plot the Quarter field on the Group axis, and the Sales field on the Data axis.

3 Specify the chart title as **Sales**, the Group axis title as **Quarters - 2002**, and the Data axis title as **Sales**.

4 Display the data points as values on the chart. Format the data points to include dollar signs.

5 Change the size of the data points to 11 pt. and make them bold.

6 Preview the report and compare it to Exhibit 5-8.

7 Save the report as **My quarterly sales report**.

8 Close the report.

9 Close Crystal Reports.

Tell students that they can experiment with changing the axis labels, but it isn't necessary to match the chart shown in the exhibit.

Exhibit 5-8: The Quarterly sales report bar chart of sales by quarter

Crystal Reports 9: Advanced

Course summary

This summary contains information to help you bring the course to a successful conclusion. Using this information, you will be able to:

A Use the summary text to reinforce what students have learned in class.

B Direct students to the next courses in this series (if any), and to any other resources that might help students continue to learn about Crystal Reports 9.

Topic A: Course summary

At the end of the class, use the following summary text to reinforce what students have learned. It is not intended as a script, but rather as a starting point.

Crystal Reports 9: Advanced

Unit 1

In this unit, students learned how to create and use **parameter fields** to display report data based on a value entered by the user. Then they learned how to apply an **edit mask** to a parameter field so that it will accept formatted input. Students also learned how to create and use a **pick list**, which provides default values for a parameter field. Students also learned how to create **unlinked and linked subreports**.

Unit 2

In this unit, students learned how to organize report objects by adding **sections**. Students also learned how to **add, modify, merge,** and **delete** report sections. Next, they learned how to create **hyperlinks**. Finally, students learned how to add documents from other applications as **OLE objects**.

Unit 3

In this unit, students learned how to use a **variable** to store a value in a formula, how to use an **array** to store multiple values of the same type, and how to use a **range variable** to test whether a value lies between specified upper and lower limits. Next, students learned how to create a formula that uses **multiple functions**, and how to use the **concatenation** operator to combine different types of values into text strings. Students also learned how to use **Evaluation Time** functions to specify when a formula should be evaluated. Then, they learned how to use **For and While constructs** to execute a set of steps repeatedly based on a condition. Finally, students learned how to **create** and **modify running totals**.

Unit 4

In this unit, students learned how to use the **Crystal Dictionaries Expert** to create and modify **dictionaries**, which enable users to view only the data relevant to them. Students also learned how to **create a report** by using a dictionary. Next, they learned about **ODBC data sources**, which are used to access data from different types of databases simultaneously. Students also learned how to create a report based on ODBC data sources. Then, they learned about **SQL**, which can be used to create **queries** for retrieving data from **relational databases**. Students also learned how to use **Crystal SQL Designer** to create SQL queries either by writing statements directly or by using the **Crystal SQL Expert**. Finally, they learned how to create, modify, and delete **report alerts**.

Unit 5

In this unit, students learned how to add **charts** to a report by using the **Chart Expert**. Next, they learned how to modify charts by using the Chart Expert and the **Chart Analyzer**. Finally, they learned how to add **maps** to a report by using the **Map Expert**, as well as how to customize a map by using the **Map menu**.

Topic B: Continued learning after class

Point out to your students that it is impossible to learn to use any software effectively in a single day. To get the most out of this class, students should begin working with Crystal Reports 9 to perform real tasks as soon as possible.

Next courses in this series

This is the last course in this series.

Other resources

For more information, please visit www.course.com.

Crystal Reports 9: Advanced

Quick reference

Button	Shortcut keys	Function
📋	CTRL + **N**	Creates a new field of the selected type.
✏️	CTRL + **E**	Edits the selected field.
🔗		Inserts a hyperlink via the Format Editor dialog box.
x·2		Checks a formula for errors.
📄		In Crystal SQL Designer, opens the New Query dialog box.
>>		Adds all fields.
>		Adds the selected field.
💾 Save and close		Saves the formula and closes the Formula Editor window.
✓ Close		Saves the formula and closes the Formula Editor window.
▶		Displays the next page of a report.
◀		Displays the first page of a report.
...		Displays the Open dialog box.
💾		Opens the File Save As dialog box.
📇		Opens the Choose Database File dialog box.

Button	Shortcut keys	Function
		Opens the Log On Server dialog box.
		Opens the Create SQL Expert dialog box.
		Opens the Choose SQL Table dialog box.

Index

A

Arrays, 3-7
    Elements of, 3-7

C

Chart Expert, 5-2, 5-6
Chart menu, 5-6
Charts
    Creating, 5-2
    Modifying, 5-6
    Templates for, 5-6
    Types of, 5-2
Clauses
    Defined, 4-16
    FROM, 4-16
    ORDER BY, 4-17
    SELECT, 4-16
    WHERE, 4-17
Concatenation operator (&), 3-12
Condition tests, 3-18
Conditional formatting formulas, 2-7
Constructs
    Defined, 3-18
    For, 3-18
    While, 3-22
Counter variables, 3-18
Crystal Dictionary Expert, 4-2
Crystal SQL Designer, 4-16, 4-22

D

Data points, 5-6
Data source (for ODBC), 4-12
Data types, 3-2
Database drivers, 4-12
Declaring variables, 3-2
Details sections, 2-2
Dictionaries
    Creating, 4-2
    Creating reports from, 4-8
    Defined, 4-2
    Modifying, 4-10
Discrete values, 1-2
Dot Density maps, 5-11

E

Edit masks, 1-6
Embedded OLE objects, 2-18
Evaluation Time functions, 3-14

F

For constructs, 3-18
Formulas
    Components of, 3-2
    Conditional formatting, 2-7
    Looping in, 3-18, 3-22
    Multiple functions in, 3-12
FROM clause, 4-16
Functions
    Evaluation Time, 3-14
    Multiple, 3-12

G

Global variables, 3-3
Graduated maps, 5-11

H

Hyperlinks, 2-14

I

Increments, 3-18
Initialization, 3-18

L

Linked OLE objects, 2-18
Linked subreports, 1-17
Local variables, 3-3
Looping, 3-18

M

Map Expert, 5-11
Map menu, 5-15
Maps
    Creating, 5-11
    Customizing, 5-15
    Types of, 5-11
Masking characters, 1-6
Merging sections, 2-10

O

ODBC (Open Database Connectivity)
    Data sources, 4-12
    Database drivers, 4-12
OLE objects, 2-18
On-demand subreports, 1-13
ORDER BY clause, 4-17

P

Panning cursor, 5-15
Parameter fields
    Applying edit masks to, 1-6
    Creating, 1-2
    Defined, 1-2
    Pick lists and, 1-10
Pick lists, 1-10
Printing reports, 2-13

Q

Queries
    Based on SQL syntax, 4-18, 4-22
    Creating reports with, 4-26
    Defined, 4-16

R

Range variables, 3-10
Ranged maps, 5-11
Ranges, 1-2
    Defined, 5-6
Records, displaying on separate pages, 2-13
Report alerts
    Creating, 4-28
    Deleting, 4-32
    Modifying, 4-30
Resolve Mismatch option (for maps), 5-15
Running totals
    Creating, 3-25
    Modifying, 3-28

S

Scope, 3-3
Section Expert, 2-2, 2-7, 2-10, 2-12, 2-13
Sections
    Adding, 2-2
    Blank, 2-7
    Deleting, 2-12

Merging, 2-10
Modifying, 2-7
Suppressing, 2-7
SELECT clause, 4-16
Shared variables, 3-3
SQL (Structured Query Language), 4-16
    Creating queries with, 4-18
    Syntax for, 4-16
SQL Expert, 4-22
Subreports, 3-3
    Defined, 1-13
    Linked, 1-17
    On-demand, 1-13
    Unlinked, 1-13
    Uses of, 1-2
Subscripts, 3-7

T

Templates (for charts), 5-6

U

Unlinked subreports, 1-13

V

Values, discrete, 1-2
Variables
    Arrays and, 3-7
    Counter, 3-18
    Declaring, 3-2
    For data types, 3-2
    Global, 3-3
    Local, 3-3
    Range, 3-10
    Scope of, 3-3
    Shared, 3-3

W

WHERE clause, 4-17
While constructs, 3-22